MW01064098

The Natural Man's Condition

A True Map of Man's Miserable Estate by Nature, Considered Either In the State of Nature or Grace

by

Christopher Love
Minister of St. Lawrence Jewry, London

Edited by Dr. Don Kistler

The Northampton Press
. . . *for instruction in righteousness* . . .

The Northampton Press
A Division of Don Kistler Ministries, Inc.
P.O. Box 781135, Orlando, FL 32878-1135
www.northamptonpress.org

*

The Natural Man's Condition was published in 1652 in
London as *A True Map of Man's Miserable Estate by Nature*.
This Northampton Press reprint, in which spelling,
grammar, and formatting changes have
been made, is © 2012 by Don Kistler.

*

ISBN 978-0-9826155-0-8

*

Library of Congress Cataloging-in-publication Data

Love, Christopher, 1618-1651.
  [True map of man's miserable estate by nature]
  The natural man's condition : a true map of man's
miserable estate by nature, considered either in the state
of nature or grace / by Christopher Love ; edited by Don
Kistler.
      p. cm.
  Originally published: A true map of man's miserable
estate by nature. London :
[s.n.], 1652.
  Includes bibliographical references and index.
  ISBN 978-0-9826155-0-8 (alk. paper)
  1. Theological anthropology–Christianity–Sermons. 2.
Theology, Doctrinal–Sermons. 3. Sermons, English–17th
century. I. Kistler, Don. II. Title.
  BT701.3.L68 2010
  248.2'4–dc22

                                      2009053485

Contents

To the Reader

The exuberant spawns of illiterate books proceeding from the polluted wombs of the overloaded and bejaded adulterate presses, which are all painted with fair titles, I compare to a cheating lottery which, when the greedy invader comes with hopes for a little money laid down to carry away a great deal of wit with him, it is at least nineteen to one when he opens it but he finds to his shame that he has drawn a blank, perhaps a blasphemy, and yet couched under the title of glorious truth, heavenly discoveries, beams of light, new Jerusalem, God's mind clearly revealed, with multitudes of such paints upon their strumpet faces.

The sacred Bible, which indeed is like an alabaster box of sweet perfumes and precious ointments, is made (alas!) like Pandora's box (in the human story, which, Epimetheus presumptuously opening, filled the world with evils, diseases, and calamities of all kinds). The sacred Bible is now made the patron of profane men's practices; never were gross sins at such an impudent height as they are now. What horrid impudence is that of hell to take heaven by the hand? Sins that were wont to hide themselves in the holes and clefts of obscurity, not daring to behold the light, but serpent-like to creep under the low shrubs of deceitful shifts, how do they sit eagle-like, perching on the goodly cedars (I mean pulpits and thrones), the cedars of God, and dare to cast up their eyes towards the sun? Who would think it! Yet what in this day is more common than to meet the devil with his eyes towards heaven and a Bible under his arm, clothing all his words and actions in Scripture phrases. Murderers, traitors, rebels, blasphemers, soothsayers, adulterers, Sabbath-breakers, perjurers, oppressors, and almost all notorious villains have marshaled themselves (like the Roman clergy) into so many several sects of religion, all impudently assuming to themselves the usurped title of eminent saints, quoting Scripture for

their actions, and so scot-free pass the press into the world
to make more proselytes. So he who in this soul-frozen age
goes to gather books to warm his soul (as Paul did sticks to
warm his fingers) will be sure, if he is not wary, to gather
vipers into his bosom. How I am stung with pain and horror while I meditate on the thousands of poor souls who
are gnawed to death by these speckled vipers! Surely it
cannot but sit sad one day upon the spirit of these licen-
tious men who are as the midwives of such monsters.

For your comfort and encouragement, therefore,
reader, I assure you this book is free from all such venomous beasts; no toad of malice or serpent of deceit lurks
either in the matter or the phrase thereof. In plain English, it is a pleasant, heavenly, self-searching, soul-
convincing, sin-condemning, heart-humbling, spirit-
raising, grace-quickening, Christ-exalting book. I need say
no more; they are the sermons of Christopher Love, minister of the gospel of Christ, whose actions, life, and death,
will eternalize his name.

The subject of these sermons is of general use to all
sorts of people, much like in that, to that text of
Chrysostom's in Psalm 4:2, which, as he said, if he had a
voice like thunder, and a mighty mountain for his pulpit,
and all the men and women in the world for his audience,
he would choose this text to preach on: "O ye sons of
men, how long will ye turn My glory into shame? How
long will ye love vanity, and seek after leasing?" Had this
really been effected, and I had been there in Mr. Love's
spirit, would Chrysostom have lent me his voice and allowed me the use of his monarchical pulpit when he had
done in the morning with his text, I would have come up
in the evening with the text of Ephesians 2:12: "at that
time ye were without Christ, being aliens from the commonwealth of Israel, and strangers from the covenants of
promise, having no hope, and without God in the world."
But this need not, for it is in a manner effected already.

This worthy minister has ascended that pulpit from
which he thundered to the world. He is now one of those
blessed ones who died in and for the Lord. He is at rest

from all his labors, and now his works follow him. Some are already gone before; these follow after.

These sermons were preached at St. Anne's, Aldersgate, where this holy young man was pastor. I pray God that they may prove as the great trumpet of God to cause a spiritual resurrection among those people before they go down to the house of rottenness. It cannot but much rejoice those people to hear their pastor's voice again; those sheep cannot but know their shepherd's voice, which, that they may do, the Lord of heaven bless his worthy labors to theirs and your spiritual advantage, so that the distressed church's loss in his sad and unexpected absence may be made up in the blessing of God upon these and the rest of his pious and painful labors. So prays,

Edmund Calamy

1

Introduction

"That at that time ye were without Christ, being aliens from the commonwealth of Israel, and strangers from the covenants of promise, having no hope, and without God in the world." Ephesians 2:12

The chapter out of which my text is taken is like a little map, containing in it a description of the little world man, and that in a double capacity, considering man either in the state of grace or in the state of nature. If you consider man in the first capacity, in the state of grace, this chapter lays down a five-fold description of bringing man into the state of grace:

1. Here is laid down the efficient cause of bringing man out of the state of nature into the state of grace, and that is God, verse 4.

2. Here is laid down the impulsive cause, and that is the riches of God's mercy in the same verse, "But God, who is rich in mercy, for His great love wherewith He loved us."

3. Here is laid down the meritorious cause of it, which is Christ in His sufferings. Verse 7: "That in the ages to come He might show the exceeding riches of His grace in His kindness toward us through Christ Jesus."

4. Here is laid down the final cause of it in the same verse also: "That in the ages to come He might show the exceeding riches of His grace."

5. Last, here is the instrumental cause of bringing man out of the state of nature into the state of grace: faith. Verse 8: "For by grace are ye saved through faith; and that not of yourselves: it is the gift of God."

The other part of the map describes man in the second capacity, in the state of nature; and herein it gives a twofold description of man's condition: positively, what he is; and privatively, what he wants.

It describes man in the state of nature positively, what he is, and that in five particulars:

1. Men in their natural condition are described as being dead in trespasses and sins.

2. They walk according to the course of this world, as pagans and heathens do.

3. They walk according to the prince of the power of the air, that is, the devil. Now the devil is called the prince of the air, either because he resides in the air, or else because he has the power of the wind and of the air.

4. They are called children of disobedience, that is, born in a state of disobedience, quite contrary to the commands of God.

5. They fulfill the lusts of the flesh and of the mind, and are by nature children of wrath. Thus far you have the positive description of man in the state of nature.

In the second place, the apostle describes him privatively, what he wants. There are, in the words of my text, five particulars wherein he plainly shows that he is the poorest man and most miserable in the world who wants Jesus Christ: "That at that time you were without Christ," that is the first; "you were aliens from the commonwealth of Israel," that is the second; "you were strangers to the covenants of promise," that is the third; "you were without hope," that is the fourth; and "you were without God in the world," that is the fifth.

Now these comprehensive expressions contain in them the whole misery of man, and that in these five particulars here named. Here is described the time how long a man is in this condition, that at that time, that is, the time during our unconverted state; as long as you are unconverted, as long you are without Christ, alienated from the commonwealth of Israel, and a stranger to the covenants of promise, without hope and without God in the world.

What a dismal text have I here to handle, and what a doleful tragedy am I now to act! But yet, out of every one of these, there is a great deal of comfort which may flow forth. I shall only at present make entrance into the words, and speak more fully to them afterwards. "That at that time you were without Christ." Beloved, here wants something to supply the sense of the words, and therefore read the foregoing words and you will find what must be brought in. The verse before runs thus: "Wherefore remember, that you being in times past Gentiles in the flesh." These words must be prefixed: "Wherefore remember, that at that time you were without Christ, and aliens to the commonwealth of Israel." I shall here, by the way, only draw out this one doctrine from the coherence of the words: "Wherefore remember that at that time." The apostle would have these converted Ephesians to remember that they were men without Christ, aliens to the commonwealth of Israel, strangers to the covenants of promise, without hope, and without God in the world. Now from hence I would commend this observation to you:

DOCTRINE. It is the will of God that men in a converted state should often call to mind the sinfulness and misery they were guilty of before their conversion.

Beloved, this is a subject I could never have occasion to speak to you of before, and yet it is a point of admirable use, especially in these times wherein people think that once they are brought into a state of grace, they must live in divine raptures, revelations, and spiritual joys, above duties and ordinances, and never look back into their former sinfulness and wickedness of which they were guilty before their conversion. Why, the Ephesians were converted men, and had extraordinary privileges; they were brought to sit in heavenly places in Christ Jesus; and yet the apostle bids them remember their former sinfulness and misery. "Remember, O you Ephesians, that you were once without Christ, and you were aliens to the commonwealth of Israel." Therefore you must take heed to not think that when you are converted, you must be only rapt up into the third heavens and never look back into your former condition; you see here the Apostle bids you remember what you were at that time during your unconverted state, that you were without Christ, strangers to the covenants of promise. So you see it is the will of God that men in a converted state should often call to mind the sins and misery they were in before conversion.

Now before I come to give you the reasons of the point, give me leave to premise these three cautions. When I tell you that after your conversion you should call to mind your sin and misery before conversion, you must not do it with complacency of spirit, nor with stupidity of heart, nor with despondency of mind.

1. You must not call to mind your former sinfulness with complacency of spirit, to please your temperaments; you must not do as some great men use to do, who have been guilty of great and crying sins such as adultery, drunkenness, swearing, and the like, in their youth, who tell and boast of them in their age. This is a very great wickedness.

You must call to mind your former sinfulness not with complacency, but with bitterness of spirit, with grief, sorrow, and perplexity of heart. Many men will tell you long stories of the wickedness they have committed, but they do it with delight; and if they had strength and abilities they would be guilty of the same sins and wickednesses still. This is a most ungodly practice, and that for which the Scripture condemns men. Ezekiel 23:19–21: "Yet she multiplied her whoredoms, in calling to remembrance the days of her youth, wherein she had played the harlot in the land of Egypt. . . . Thus thou calledst to remembrance the lewdness of thy youth." The meaning is this: she called her sins to remembrance, but it was so as to play the whore and be unclean still; she did it with delight and complacency, with content and joy. Now I say, you should call your sins to remembrance with a great deal of grief, sorrow, and bitterness of spirit. And therefore, when young gallants will boast of their sins, and tell how often they have played the whoremaster, and draw others to do so, this is a most diabolical remembrance.

2. You must not call your former sins to remembrance with stupidity of heart either. Beloved, there are many

men who can remember what lewd courses they have taken, and what wicked lives they have lived—how often they have been drunk and unclean, and the like—and yet they are never troubled at the remembrance of it. Their hearts do not smite them with remorse and sorrow, but are like a rock. The sense of sin never troubles them. This is no way to call sin to remembrance, with a blockish and stupid heart; that is not thanks worthy. But it must be done with a broken, a bleeding, and contrite heart.

3. Take in this caution too: it must not be done with despondency of mind either. There are many converted ones who call their sins to remembrance, but it makes them discouraged and unwilling to come to Christ; it makes them think that they have no interest in the covenant of grace. But this should not be. The true effect that the consideration of your former sinfulness should produce should be to lay your souls low and make them humble, and more sensible of that indispensable need you have of Christ, of going to Him for salvation and comfort.

These are the cautions necessary to be premised.

I come now to give you the reasons of the point why it is the will of God that people in a converted state should often call to mind the sin and misery they were in before conversion.

REASON 1. God will have it so because, by so doing, you will be provoked more highly to magnify and admire the greatness and riches of God's grace and mercy, than those who are most studious of their own sin and misery. You will never solemnly and thoroughly magnify God's mercy till you are plunged into a deep sensibleness of your own misery, till the Lord has brought you to see in what a miserable and deplorable condition you were in before conversion. You will then admire and magnify the riches of God's free grace in bringing you out of that condition into the state of grace, as in 1 Timothy 1:13. The Apostle Paul, when he would magnify the free grace of God to him, said, "I was a blasphemer, and a persecutor, and injurious; and yet through the abundance of God's free grace and mercy, I have obtained mercy." The con-

sideration of his former sinfulness elevated and drew up
his heart to make him admire the free grace of God to his
soul. That man can never prize liberty as he should who
never was in prison.

REASON 2. Another reason why God will have it so is
because this will be a spur to quicken and engage men to
be more eminent in grace after their conversion. When a
man frequently and seriously considers how bad and sinful he was before conversion, it cannot but provoke him
now to be more humble and holy after his conversion. It is
very observable in Paul that all those sins and wickednesses he was guilty of before conversion he strove most of
all against, and labored to excel in the contrary graces after conversion. Before conversion, he labored to haul
others to prison for worshiping Christ; but after his conversion he labored to draw others to Christ. Acts 26:10–11:
"Many of the saints did I shut up in prison. . .and gave my
voice against them, and punished them oft in every syna-
gogue, and being exceedingly mad against them, I persecuted them even unto strange cities." And now you shall
see that after conversion Paul labored to outvie in grace
the evil course he was in before conversion. He impris-
oned those who belonged to Christ, so after conversion he
was shut up himself in prison for the cause of Christ. Before conversion he gave his voice against the people of
God, but after conversion he prayed to God for them. Before conversion he punished them often, but afterward he
preached to them often. Before conversion he compelled
men to blaspheme Christ, but after conversion he was very
earnest to persuade people to believe in Christ. He was
exceeding mad against them before conversion, but afterward he was so exceeding zealous for the people of God;
everyone thought he had been mad. And last, before conversion he persecuted saints to strange cities, but afterwards he went preaching the gospel to strange cities. O
my beloved, let Paul's pattern be your task: call to mind
your sin and wickedness in your unconverted condition,
but so that it may provoke you; that now you are converted, you may labor to abound in grace as formerly you

have abounded in sin.

REASON 3. Another reason why God will have us call to mind the sin and misery we were in before conversion is because this will be a means to kindle a great deal of pity and compassion in our souls towards those who remain yet unconverted. This the apostle exhorts us to in Titus 3:2–3: "Speak evil of no man, be no brawlers, but gentle, showing all meekness unto all men. For we ourselves also were sometime foolish, disobedient, deceived, serving divers lusts and pleasures, living in malice and envy, hateful, and hating one another." It is as if the apostle had said, "I, Paul, and you, Titus, were sinful as well as they, and served divers lusts as well as they once did; let us therefore be pitiful, merciful, and compassionate towards them." This consideration will greatly provoke us to commiserate poor sinful souls; the great reason why we pity them no more than we do is because we do not call to mind our own sinfulness, and what we were before conversion.

REASON 4. Another reason may be because the consideration of our former misery will greatly abate pride in the hearts of converted men. This will be a great means to abate and keep under pride, and advance humility in the hearts of God's people. Beloved, a good man naturally is apt to be proud; we are not proud of our sins, but of our graces. Pride is apt to grow in the best man's heart, and therefore God would have us sometimes look back upon what we were in our unconverted state so that it might abate the pride of our spirits. You have an excellent place for this in Ezekiel 16:3–5 compared with the last verse of that chapter. God says there to Jerusalem: "Thy birth and thy nativity is of the land of Canaan; thy father was an Amorite, and thy mother an Hittite. And as for thy nativity, in the day thou wast born. . .thy navel was not cut, neither wast thou washed in water to supple thee. . . . None eye pitied thee to do any of these unto thee. . .but thou wast cast out into the open field, to the loathing of thy person in the day that thou wast born. That thou mayest remember and be confounded, and never open thy mouth any more, because of thy shame, when I am pacified toward thee for all that thou hast done, saith the Lord God." They must remember their guilt and shame when God is pacified towards them, and when God is reconciled to them.

You have another place for the same purpose in Ezekiel 20:43: "And there shall you remember your ways, and all your doings, wherein you have been defiled, and you shall loathe yourselves in your sight, for all the evil that you have committed." I remember what Plutarch related of one Agathocles, who was advanced from a porter's son, a low, a mean, and contemptible condition, to be king of Sicily. This man, when he might have been served every day in golden dishes, yet would still have his provisions brought in earthen dishes because, he said, "I may remember what I was, and what I am, a potter's son, that so I may not be too much lifted up and exalted." Remember what you were, your father a potter and you a poor, miserable, sinful creature, and this will abate the pride of your hearts.

REASON 5. Last, God would have us call to mind our former sinfulness because this will make us more watchful and circumspect, so that we do not run again into those sins that we were guilty of before conversion. God would not have us do it to drive us to despair, or to question our evidences for heaven, but to make us humble and watchful, so that we run not again into the same sins. You may thus think with yourself: "Before conversion I spent my days in sin and wickedness, and consumed my years in vanity and pleasures, fulfilling the lusts of the flesh and of the mind." And the consideration of this will lay an engagement upon your soul to walk more carefully, prudently, and holily in time to come. The apostle makes use of this in Ephesians 5:8: "Ye were sometimes darkness, but now are ye light in the Lord; walk therefore as children of the light." We should now hate and abhor those sins that formerly we have delighted in.

These are the reasons of the point. I shall only make one short use of it; which shall be of reprehension to those who (notwithstanding it is the will of God, that men after conversion should call to mind the sin they were guilty of before conversion) yet cross this doctrine either in judgment or practice.

This reproves those who contradict this doctrine in their judgment, and think that once they are converted they must never look back upon their former wretchedness, but only live in divine raptures, revelations, spiritual joys, and comforts. For if Paul's precept has warrant, then this opinion has no warrant; for he tells us that we must remember what we were in our unconverted state, that we were at that time without Christ, without hope, and without God in the world. Paul told the Ephesians that were an elect people, elected before the beginning of the world, that they must remember that they were dead in trespasses and sins heretofore, though now they were quickened. And if Paul bids them call to mind their former sinfulness, then why should not we do it?

This reproves those who, though they do not deny this doctrine in judgment, yet do not make it their practice to call to mind their former sins that they were guilty of before conversion. I dare warrant that many of you can remember what you have done, and what debts have been owed to you for twenty years, but yet cannot call to mind what sins you committed twenty years ago. It may be that some of you have been cheaters and swearers, adulterers, and profaners, and yet now you never think of it, but imagine all is well. I do not know how to express what a sad, dismal, and deplorable condition your poor soul is in, you who never call to mind your former sins.

2

What It Is to Be Without Christ

"That at that time ye were without Christ."
Ephesians 2:12

We come now to the body and bulk of the work, "That at that time ye were without Christ."

DOCTRINE. Every man, during the time of his unregeneracy, is in a condition without Jesus Christ.

My beloved, if I should tell you now that when you come home you would never have a bit of bread to put in your mouths, that all your subsistence and livelihood would be taken away, that you would be heirs of never a foot of land, and that you would have nothing at all to live upon, you would count this a hard case; but I tell you, my brethren, that to be without Jesus Christ is a far worse case. It is the saddest and most miserable thing in the world to be without Jesus Christ. When I tell you, that you are without Christ, I tell you the saddest news in the world; but before I can bring home this doctrine to you, there is one objection and one question that I must spend a little time in answering.

OBJECTION. How can it be said of these Ephesians who were elect that before their conversion they were without Jesus Christ, for they were "chosen of God in Christ before the world was made"? And therefore, how can the apostle say that when they were born they were without Jesus Christ, seeing they were chosen in Christ before the beginning of the world?

ANSWER. I answer that the same man, in a different sense, may be said both to be in Christ and out of Christ. It is true, the apostle says, first, that they were chosen in Christ before the world was.

10

If you respect the eternal decree and determination of God, they were in Christ, for God purposed to make Jesus Christ a Mediator between God and man, by whose blood they should be saved.

Though they were in Christ in regard of God's decree, yet they were without Christ in regard of the application of the blood of Christ to their souls. For till a man has faith, he can make no application of the love of God to him; for he who has not the Spirit of Christ is none of His. Though they were in Christ in regard of the eternal decree of God, yet they were without Christ in regard of the actual application of the love of God to them; for they could not apply to their own souls that Christ loved and owned them as his children till they were brought into a converted state.

I come now to the question I promised to resolve:

QUESTION. What it is to be without Christ?

ANSWER. It includes in it these three things: to be without the saving knowledge of Christ, to be without any actual interest in Christ, and to be without any spiritual communion with Christ.

Now if you ask me which of these is chiefly meant that these Ephesians were without, I answer the two former, for they were both without the true knowledge of Christ and also without any actual interest in Christ.

To be without Christ is to be without the saving knowledge of Jesus Christ. Though a man, during his unconverted state, may gather together a great deal of notional knowledge, yet the Scripture lays him under this condition: he is a man without Christ. Now a man may be said to be without the knowledge of Christ in these five particulars:

1. A man may have a common knowledge of Christ, and yet be without spiritual knowledge of Christ. He may have a natural knowledge by the works of God, by hearing, reading, or the like, and yet be without a spiritual knowledge to know Christ in a spiritual manner.

2. A man may have a notional knowledge, and yet be without an experimental knowledge of Christ. Hence it is

the Scripture expresses the difference between the knowledge of the righteous and of the wicked man: the Lord
plants wisdom in the secret parts of His children, but only
in the outward parts, in the head and in the brain of
wicked men. God makes His children to know Christ in
the inward parts.

3. An unregenerate man may have a contemplative
knowledge, and yet be without an effective knowledge of
Jesus Christ. Wicked men may have a speculative knowledge of Christ, they may know Christ as a man knows his
neighbor, but a believer knows Christ as a wife knows her
husband. A believer knows Christ, and he loves Christ too.
An unregenerate man may have much light, but he has
but little heat in his knowledge. He may grow much in a
contemplative knowledge, but not in an effective knowledge. He knows what he should do, but he will not do
what he knows. A wicked man's knowledge is like the
moon: it has light with it but no heat. But a godly man's
knowledge is like the sun: it has heat as well as light; a believer loves Christ as well as knows Him.

4. An unregenerate man is without an appropriating
knowledge of Christ. He does not know Christ to be his
Christ; there are none who know Christ to be theirs but
those who belong to Christ. Now in this sense, a man may
be a great knowing man and yet not know Jesus Christ.

5. Last, an unregenerate man is without a practical
knowledge of Jesus Christ. He knows much, but does little.
Titus 1:16 says that "In their words they profess to know
Him, but in their works they deny Him." Though they
know God, yet they do not glorify Him as God; they know
many things, but will do nothing. Now put all these together: an unregenerate man is without the knowledge of
Christ; he is without a spiritual and experimental knowledge; he is without an effective and apprehensive knowledge; and he is without an appropriating and practical
knowledge of Christ.

To be without Christ implies not only to be without a
saving knowledge of Christ, but also to be without an actual interest in Christ. "That at that time ye were without

Christ," that is, during the time of your unconverted state, you were without any real actual interest in Christ. From whence observe:

DOCTRINE. Every man, during the time of his unregeneracy, is without any actual interest in Christ.

In handling this point, I shall only do three things:

I shall show you the properties of a man without Christ;

I shall show you the characters of a man without Christ; and

I shall show you the misery of a man without Christ, and then come to the uses.

I shall show you the properties of a man without Christ. And in treating this subject, I wish from my soul that if I cannot allure you, yet I might frighten and thoroughly awaken you to see the indispensable need that you have of getting an interest in Jesus Christ. Here I shall discover to you eight particular properties of a man without Christ:

Every man without Jesus Christ is a base man.

He is a bondman.

He is a beggarly man.

He is a blind man.

He is a deformed man.

He is a disconsolate man.

He is a dead man.

He is a damned man.

These are the eight properties of a man without Jesus Christ.

Every man without Jesus Christ is a base man. Though you are born of the blood of nobles, and though you are of the offspring of princes, yet if you have not the royal blood of Jesus Christ running in your veins, you are a base man. In Daniel 11:21 and Psalm 15:4, you read of vile persons. Such is every man without Christ: and he must be so because only Christ can take off that baseness wherein every one is by nature. In Isaiah 43:4 God says, "Since thou wast precious in my sight, thou hast been honorable," and 1 Peter 2:7 says, "Unto you therefore which believe, Christ

is precious." It is Jesus Christ who puts a diamond of
honor and glory upon men. They are all base men that
are out of Jesus Christ, and that in these three respects:

They come from a base origin.

They commit base actions.

And they aim at base ends.

For the first respect, every man who is out of Christ
comes from a base origin. He does not have his origin
from the Spirit, but from the flesh; he proceeds not from
God who is the Father of lights, but from the devil who is
the prince of darkness.

Second, he is base because he commits base actions.
All the actions and services of a Christless man are at best
as but filthy rags and dead works. A man, in his unconverted state, is the slave and drudge of the devil, a worker
of wickedness still fulfilling the desires of the flesh and of
the mind, being given over to vile affections.

Third, he is a base man without Christ because he aims
at base ends in whatever he does, and that two ways: In
this world he aims at base ends in his hearing, reading,
praying, and profession of religion; he minds himself and
his own ends in all. All his actions tend to base ends in
another world; as the actions of a man in Christ tend to
salvation, so the actions of a Christless man tend to damnation.

A man without Christ is not only a base man, but a
bondman. This Christ told us of in John 8:36: "If the Son
shall make you free, then are you free indeed," intimating,
that if you have not an interest in Christ to free you from
the slavery of sin and Satan, you are slaves indeed. This
bondage and slavery likewise consists in three particulars:
They are slaves to sin, slaves to the devil, and slaves to the
law.

Every Christless man is a slave to sin. In John 8:34
Christ says, "Verily I say unto you, whosoever committeth
sin is the servant of sin," and 2 Peter 2:19 says, "While they
promise them liberty, they themselves are servants of corruption, for of whom a man is overcome, of the same he is
brought in bondage." Every man by nature is a slave to his

lusts, a slave to sin, and to the creatures. God made man lord over all the creatures, but man has made himself servant to all the creatures.

A Christless man is not only in bondage and slavery to sin, but to the devil too. 2 Timothy 2, the two last verses, says, "In meekness instructing those that oppose themselves, if God peradventure will give them repentance, to the acknowledging of the truth, and that they may recover themselves out of the snare of the devil, who are taken captive by him at his will."

A Christless man is in bondage to the law, that is, he does nothing in obedience to the law. And this is the great misery of a man without Christ: he is bound to keep the whole law of God. There is a very strange expression in Revelation. John tells us that all those who did worship the beast, shall cry, "Woe and alas, for Babylon is fallen," and shall cry for the slaves and souls of men. All wicked men are slaves to antichrist, to sin, and to the law; and this is the great misery of an unregenerate man.

You are not only a base and a bondman, but a beggarly man too, without Jesus Christ. For all the treasures of grace and mercy are hidden and locked up in Christ as in a common magazine or store house. Colossians 2:3: "In Him are hid all the treasures of wisdom and knowledge." If you are out of Christ you have nothing. Revelation 3:17: "Thou sayest thou art rich and increased in goods, and hast need of nothing, and knowest not that thou art poor, and wretched, and miserable, and blind, and naked." You will grant that he is a poor and beggarly man who lacks these four things: meat for his belly, clothes for his back, money for his purse, and a house to put his head in. Why, in all these respects, every man who is out of Christ is a beggarly man.

A beggarly man is one who has no meat to put in his belly; and all you who have no interest in Jesus Christ are beggarly in this regard because you do not feed upon that bread of life, nor drink of that water of life, the Lord Christ, whose flesh is meat indeed and whose blood is drink indeed, without which your souls will starve.

You will say he is a poor man who has no clothes to put on his back. Thus every man out of Christ is not only poor, but naked. Revelation 3:17: "Thou knewest not that thou wert poor and miserable, and blind and naked." That man who is not clothed with the long robes of Christ's righteousness is a naked man, exposed to the wrath and vengeance of Almighty God. Those men have only a cloak to cover their sinful nakedness and shame who are clothed with the robes of Christ's righteousness. It is said that Jacob obtained the blessing from his father by being clad in the garments of his eldest brother; and so are we only blessed by God our Father as we are clothed with the robes of our elder brother Jesus Christ.

That man is a beggarly man who has no money in his purse. So, though your purses are full of gold, yet if your hearts are not full of grace, you are very beggarly men, Luke 16:11. Grace is only the true riches; all the durable riches are bound up in Christ.

Lastly, he is a beggarly man who has no house to put his head in, who is destitute of a house to lodge in, and a bed to lie on. So you who have no interest in Christ, when your days are expired and death comes, you know not what to do, nor where to go. You cannot say with the godly man that when death takes you hence you shall be received into everlasting habitations; you cannot say that Christ has gone before to prepare a place for you in heaven.

So in these four particulars you see that a Christless man is a very beggarly man, having neither food for his body, nor clothes for his back, nor money in his purse, nor a house to put his head in, unless it is in a dungeon of darkness with devils and damned spirits.

Another property of a man without Christ is that he is a blind man. Revelation 3:17: "And knowest not that thou art wretched, and miserable, and poor, and blind, and naked," and hence it is that wicked men, during their unregeneracy, are called darkness. Ephesians 5:8: "Ye were sometimes darkness, but now are ye light in the Lord; walk as children of light." So light has come into the world, and yet men love darkness rather than light because "their deeds are evil." Jesus Christ is to the soul what the sun is to the earth. Take away the sun from the earth and it is nothing but a dungeon of darkness; take away Christ from the soul and it is nothing but a dungeon of the devil. Though there is a Christ in the world, yet if the heart is shut, and Jesus Christ is not in you, you are in a state of darkness and blindness.

Every man without Christ is a deformed man, as you may read in Ezekiel 16:3–6, 8, 11, and 14th verses: "Thus saith the Lord God, thy nativity is in the land of Canaan, thy father was an Amorite." And in the 6th verse: "When I passed by thee, and saw thee polluted in thine own blood, I said unto thee (when thou wast in thy blood), Live, yea, I said unto thee, when thou wast in thy blood, Live." When a poor child lies weltering in its blood, not swaddled, nor washed, nor looked after, what a sad condition is it in! And thus were you, says God. But then read on in the 7th verse: "I have caused thee to multiply as the bud of the field, and thou hast increased and waxen great." And so again in the 14th verse: "Thy renown went forth among the heathen for thy beauty; for it was perfect through My comeliness which I had put upon thee," said the Lord; intimating that before Christ looks upon a soul, he lies weltering in his own blood, unable to help himself; but he becomes comely through Christ's comeliness that is cast upon him. If you lack Christ, you lack your best ornament. A man without Christ is like a body full of sores and botches; he is like a dark house without light, and like a body without a head; and such a man must needs be a deformed man.

Another property of a Christless man is that he is a disconsolate man. Christ is the only spring of comfort, and the fountain of all joy and consolation. Take away Christ from the soul, and it is as if you took away the sun from the firmament. If a man has all the blessings in the world, yet if he wants Christ he wants that which would sweeten all the rest of his comforts. In Exodus 15:23–25, you read of the waters of Marah: they were so bitter that none could drink of them; but then the Lord showed Moses a tree that, when he had cast into the waters, the waters were made sweet. Why, Jesus Christ is this tree that sweetens the bitterness of any outward affliction. He can make all your sorrows to fly away. There is nothing in the world that sweetens the comforts, and gives us joy in the possession of the things of this world, more than the having an interest in Jesus Christ. It is not, beloved, having much of the creature in our house, but having Christ in your hearts that makes you live comfortably. All the bread you eat will be but the bread of sorrow if you do not feed upon the body of Jesus Christ; and all your drink will be but the wine of astonishment if you do not drink of the blood of Jesus Christ. Without an interest in Christ, all your comforts are but crosses, and all your mercies are but miseries. Job 20:22: "In the fullness of his sufficiency he shall be in straits." Though you have an abundance of the things of this life, though you have more than enough, yet if you have not an interest in Christ you have nothing.

Another property of a man out of Christ is that he is a dead man. You know that common place in 1 John 5:12: "He that hath the Son hath life, and he that hath not the Son of God hath not life." Hence we read in Ephesians 2:1 that unregenerate men are dead in trespasses and sins, and the reason is because Christ is a believer's life. Colossians 3:3: "Your life is hid with Christ in God." Take away Christ from a man and you take away his life; and take away life from a man and he is a dead lump of flesh. Unregenerate men are termed strangers to the life of godliness, and therefore must be dead in their sins. Though they enjoy the life of a man, yet if the life that he lives is not by the faith of the Son of God, he is spiritually dead. For example, you know a dead man feels nothing; do what you will to him, he does not feel it. So a man who is spiritually dead does not feel the weight of his sins, though they are a heavy burden pressing him down into the pit of hell. He is a stranger to the life of godliness, and past feeling, given over to a reprobate sense, so that he feels not the weight and burden of all his sins.

A dead man has a title to nothing here in this life. Though he is ever so rich, yet he loses his title to all, and his riches go from him to another. So, being spiritually dead, you can lay claim to nothing, neither to grace, nor mercy, heaven, or happiness by Jesus Christ.

A dead man is still rotting and returning to the dust from whence he came; and so a man who is spiritually dead falls from iniquity to iniquity, and from one sin to another, till at last he drops down into hell fire.

The last property of a Christless man is that he is a damned man; if he lives and dies without Christ, he is a damned man. John 3:18: "He that believeth not is condemned already." He is as surely damned as if he were in hell already. He who is without Jesus Christ must go without heaven, for heaven and glory and happiness are entailed upon Him. Heaven is given to none but those who are heirs together with Christ; and therefore, you who are without Christ must be without heaven, and consequently without happiness and salvation, and therefore must be damned.

So you see, in these eight particular properties, in what a sad and miserable condition every Christless man is in; and Oh, that what has been now declared, concerning the wretchedness of a Christless man, might provoke every soul to a holy eagerness and earnestness of spirit! Above all your "gettings," labor to get Jesus Christ!

3

The Characteristics of a Man Without Jesus Christ

"That at that time ye were without Christ."
Ephesians 2:12

We come now to the second question, which I promised you I would resolve.

QUESTION. What are the characteristics of a man without Jesus Christ?

ANSWER. This question is very necessary, because hereby we may know whether we are the men who are without Jesus Christ or not. Now I shall reduce these characters of a Christless man into these seven heads, and go over them very briefly.

1. The man who is without the Spirit of Christ is without any real actual interest in Christ. This the apostle lays down to us in so many expressed terms in Romans 8:9: "If any man hath not the Spirit of Christ, he is none of His." Christ and the Spirit are inseparable companions; have the one and you enjoy the other; want the one and you are without the other. And here, beloved, to apply this more particularly, you are without any interest in Christ if you are without the Spirit of Christ in the threefold operation of it:

If you are without the enlightening work of the Spirit to teach your minds to know Christ;

If you are without the inclining work of the Spirit to draw your hearts to love Christ; and

If you are without the constraining work of the Spirit to empower your wills to obey Christ.

If you are thus without the Spirit of Christ in these three particulars, you can lay no just claim to any interest in Jesus Christ. With what face therefore can any of you lay claim to Christ's person who are not guided by His Spirit, but are led by the corrupt dictates of your own hearts, and follow the desires of the flesh and of the mind? You who are thus can lay no claim to Jesus Christ, for whoever has not the Spirit of Christ is none of his. This is the first character.

2. He who is without any saving power derived from Jesus Christ, enabling him to mortify his bosom lusts, that man is without Jesus Christ. In Galatians 5:24, the apostle tells us: "They that are Christ's have crucified the flesh with the affections and lusts," thereby intimating that they who have *not* crucified the flesh with the affections and lusts thereof have no interest in the Lord Jesus Christ. When Christ came in the flesh, we crucified Him; but if ever Christ comes into your soul, He will crucify you! Those who are Christ's crucify the flesh. Christ will be avenged on your sins, crucify your lusts, and kill your corruptions when He comes into your soul. But here, beloved, I do not mean a total subduing of sin, as if every lust and corruption should be quite subdued; but only so far as to give a deadly blow to sin; that sin shall not reign nor bear sway in your soul as it has done formerly. Sin in the heart of one who is in Christ shall be like those monarchs spoken of in Daniel 7:12. It is said, "They had their dominion taken away, yet their lives were prolonged for a season and a time." Just so it is with sin in the heart of a believer; the dominion of sin is taken away, but the life and being of it is preserved for a little season. There shall be some remainders of sin still in the best of God's servants, but sin shall not reign in their mortal bodies; and therefore you who never had any power to mortify your sins, who never had any bridle of restraint to any of your lusts, lay no claim to Jesus Christ, for they that are His have crucified the flesh with the lusts thereof. I might here make use of a story (that I have often told you of) in the history of Scotland. There is mention made of an island, situated in the midst of the sea, between Scotland and Ireland; and there was a great controversy between

the two nations as to which of the kingdoms this island belonged. A great politician, to decide the controversy, commanded a great company of toads and frogs to be gathered together and put into the island, and if those venomous and unclean beasts should live there, then the island belonged to Scotland, but if they died, then it belonged to Ireland, for no unclean creature inhabits there. Just so it is with us: there is a great controversy between Christ and the devil, to whom your soul belongs. Why, now, if poisonous lusts and venomous sins can live and thrive in your soul, then you belong to the devil; but if these lusts and sins die in your soul, then you belong to Jesus Christ.

3. That man who is without unfeigned love to the person of Christ is without any interest in Christ; for everyone who has Christ loves Him, and every one who does not have Him does not love Him. 1 Corinthians 16:22: "If any man loves not the Lord Jesus Christ, let him be anathema." He who does not love Christ has no interest in Christ, and shall be accursed when Christ comes to judgment.

OBJECTION. But some will be ready to say, "If this is so, that not loving Christ is an argument of not having Christ, why, then, I think I am well enough, for I love Christ with all my heart."

ANSWER. I will tell you in the very words of Christ who loves Him. John 14:24: "He that loveth Me not keepeth not My sayings." Does not your conscience tell you, O man, that you do not care for any command of Jesus Christ? Let Him command what He will, you will do what you wish. You see here that Christ tells you plainly that he who does not love Him does not keep His sayings. I beseech you, therefore, in the fear of God, take heed of deceiving your own souls in thinking you love Christ when there is no such matter; but labor to love Him in truth, and evidence your love to Him by keeping His commandments.

4. That man who is without any saving knowledge of Christ is without any actual interest in Christ. There is no

man who has Christ but knows Christ. Mistake me not, I do not say that every man who has Christ knows he has Him, for a man may have Christ and yet not know it for the present; but this I say, he who has an interest in Christ, whoever he is, must know Christ in part. John 8:54–55: "Ye say that He is your God, yet ye have not known Him." It is a very strange place, you say that God and salvation by Him, is all yours, and yet you have not known Him. O my beloved, you say you have Christ, and yet you have not known Christ. He Himself will convinct you at the last day of laying a false claim to Him. Read John 1:12 and compare it with the 24th and 26th verses.

Now when I tell you that a man without the knowledge of Christ is without any interest in Christ, I do not say that those are without Christ who have not as great a measure of knowledge as other men have; but when you are without the knowledge of Christ, accompanied with these two circumstances, then I can safely pronounce you to be a Christless man:

First, if you are without the knowledge of Christ, and yet sit down contented in your ignorance, neither desiring nor laboring after the knowledge of Him, then I may safely say that, for the present, you are without Jesus Christ. If you are like those spoken of in 2 Peter 3:5: "For this they willingly are ignorant of, that by the word of God, the heavens were of old, and the earth standing out of the water, and in the water"; or like those in Job 21:14: "They say unto God, Depart from us; for we desire not the knowledge of Thy ways." If you are such as these, I can safely pronounce you to be Christless men.

Second, not only when you are contentedly ignorant, but likewise when, with obscurity in your judgments, you add obstinacy in your wills. You are a Christless man if you are an ignorant man, and do not know and will not know; if you have not learned and yet will not learn, but are like those spoken of in Psalm 82:5: "They know not, neither will they understand." He does not say they know not, neither *do* they, "but neither *will* they understand." A godly man may have the former of these. Although you are very

ignorant, yet if you desire to know, you may have an interest in Christ. But I am bold to say (in case you are ignorant, and yet sit down contentedly and do not care to
know more, and obstinately, and will not learn more) that
you have no interest in Christ; and therefore keep your
hands off of Christ; lay no claim to Him, for you have
nothing to do with Him. He is none of yours.

5. That man who is without a hearing ear to the voice
of Christ, and an obedient heart to the commands of
Christ, has no interest in Christ. I shall give you two plain
texts of Scripture to prove this. One is John 8:47: "He that
is of God heareth God's words; ye therefore hear them
not, because ye are not of God." Those who are of God
hear His Word; those who belong to Christ, and have an
interest in Him, hear His Word not only with the ear, but
with the heart. And so in 1 John 4:6 the apostle says, "We
are of God; he that knoweth God heareth us; he that is
not of God heareth not us; hereby know we the spirit of
truth and the spirit of error." And therefore, you obstinate
and stout-hearted wretch who can lie like a flint under the
Word of God, and suffer no command to make impres-
sion upon your spirit, verily you can lay no just claim to
Jesus Christ.

6. The man who uses greater industry, and takes
greater complacency in the acting and committing of sin,
than ever he did in the exercise of any grace or the performance of any duty, that man is without Jesus Christ.
You have an excellent place for this purpose in 1 John
3:8–10: "He that committeth sin, is of the devil." He does
not say, "He who sins is of the devil," but "he who commits
sin with delight, who makes a trace of sin, *he* is of the
devil." And so on in the 10th verse: "In this the children of
God are manifest, and the children of the devil; whosoever doeth not righteousness is not of God." He does not
belong to God: he who does not do righteousness with delight, complacency, joy, and industry. As he who commits
sin—that is, acts it with delight and makes a trade of it—is
of the devil, so he who does not do righteousness—that is,
with delight, joy, and cheerfulness—is not of Christ. You,

then, who can sin with delight, but perform holy duties with a flat, dead, and dull spirit; you who never took so much delight to sanctify the Sabbath as you have done in profaning it; you who never took so much delight in performing duties to God as you have done in sinning against God, lay off hands from Jesus Christ. If your hearts are full of sin, you can have no interest in Him. In John 9:16, some of the Pharisees said, "This man is not of God, because he keepeth not the Sabbath." This has been a very good argument whether you are of God or not: if you profane the Sabbath day, and make no conscience of performing holy duties, nor of sinning against God, this shows that you are not of God. The man who acts sin with more delight than he performs holy duties has no interest in Christ. 1 John 5:18: "Whosoever is born of God sinneth not," that is, he does not commit it with that delight and complacency that wicked men do. But he who belongs to God "keepeth himself, and that wicked one toucheth him not," that is, not so as to make him commit sin in the former sense, but he keeps himself. He will not give himself to commit sin with that cheerfulness that wicked men have; and therefore the apostle said in 1 John 5:19, "We know that we are of God, and the whole world lieth in wickedness."

7. That man is without any interest in Christ who backslides from the ways of Christ, both in judgment and in practice. Beloved, when a man shall backslide from the truth of Christ in judgment, and from the exercises of holy duties in practice, when he backslides both these ways, he is not in Jesus Christ. 2 John 1:9: "Whosoever transgresseth, and abideth not in the doctrine of Christ hath not God. He that abideth in the doctrine of Christ, he hath both the Father and the Son." The man who sins both in judgment and in practice is not of God; but he who abides in the truth of God, both in judgment and in practice, has both the Father and the Son.

Oh, therefore, I beseech you in the fear of God, look about you to see whether you are the men who have a real actual interest in Christ or not. Are you such men as are without the Spirit of Christ? Are you without a saving power derived from Christ, enabling you to mortify your bosom lusts? Are you without an unfeigned love to the person of Christ, or without a true and saving knowledge of Christ? Are you contentedly ignorant of Christ, and care not to know more? Are you obstinately ignorant, and will not learn more? Are you without a hearing ear and an obedient heart to the Word of Christ? Do you take greater industry and complacency in the committing of sin than ever you did in the performance of any holy duty? Do you backslide from the ways of Christ both in judgment and in practice? If there is a concurrence of these seven characters in you, then conclude that you have no interest at all in Christ; conclude then that at this time you are without Jesus Christ.

Thus now I have done with the second question that I promised to answer. I shall now spend a little time in winding up what I have said in a practical use, and then come to the third question. And in the application of this I shall direct my speech to two sorts of people: those who are plunged into a spiritual delusion, to say they have an interest in Christ when they have not, and to those who say they have no interest in Christ when they have.

Application

USE 1. To you who say you have an interest in Christ when you have not, give me leave to propound these three or four questions to you:

First, let me ask this question: Were you ever without Christ, yes or no? If you answer no, then let me tell you this much: that man who says he had Christ ever, I may safely say he had Christ never. You who say that you had Christ ever since you were born, I can safely say that you have *never* had Christ since you were born, for every man is born a Christless man.

Second, you who say you have an interest in Christ, let me ask you this question: How came you by your interest in Christ? Do you think that Christ fell from heaven into your bosom, whether you wanted Him to or not? How came you by Christ then? Did you ever make a powerful prayer unto God for Him? Did you ever sigh and sob and cry mightily unto God for Him? Did you ever see your misery without Him, and beg the Father earnestly for Him? God is not prodigal of His Son, to give Him to those who never ask for Him.

Third, let me ask you this question: Did you ever see an absolute necessity in your own souls of getting an interest in Jesus Christ? Were you ever sensible of the want of Christ, of the worth of Christ, of the need you have of Christ, and in what a sad, miserable, deplorable, and damnable condition you are in without Christ? If you are not sensible of this, you are to this day without Jesus Christ.

Fourth, let me ask you this question: Can you evidence that you have an interest in Christ by your walking? What does the apostle say in 2 Corinthians 5:17? "If any man be in Christ, he is a new creature; old things are passed away, and all things are become new." Are you new creatures? Are all your old sins passed away? The apostle tells you that "they that are Christ's have crucified the flesh with the affections and lusts." Why now, have you killed any lust in your heart, or, rather, does not every lust reign in you with as much power as ever they did? If it is so, then surely you have no interest in Christ at all.

USE 2. Thus much for the first sort of people, those who are plunged into a spiritual delusion. We come now to the second sort of people: those doubting and perplexed souls who say they do not have an interest in Christ when they have; those who say they are without Christ when indeed they are not without Him. As there are many such people in the world, now to such as these I have two or three words of consolation.

First, let me speak this for your comfort: it is a very ordinary thing with the people of God to pass very hard and uncharitable sentences upon their own souls, and to run upon very sad mistakes in reference to their own salvation.

A child of God sees so many lusts in his own heart, and so many sins within him, that he can scarcely have a charitable thought of his own soul. David said, "The Lord hath forsaken me, and cast me off forever." Godly men are very apt to pass very harsh censures on their own souls.

Second, let me tell you this for your comfort: you may have Christ, and yet not know that you have Him. It may be with you as it was with Mary Magdalene when she was talking to Christ face to face: "They have taken away my Lord, and I know not where they have laid Him." So you may have an interest in Christ, and yet not know it. In John 14:4, Christ told His disciples, "Whither I go ye know, and the way ye know. Thomas saith unto him, 'Lord we know not whither Thou goest; and how can we know the way?' " The reason why they did not know, as Augustine well observed, was because they did not know their own thoughts; they thought they did not know, but yet Christ knew that they *did* know. It is with a believer, sometimes, as it was with Benjamin: the cup was in his sack, and yet he did not know it. Benjamin was the beloved of Joseph; so you may be the beloved ones of Christ and yet not know it.

Third, to you who think you are without Christ when you are not, let me tell you this for your comfort: though having Christ is indispensably necessary for bringing our souls to heaven, yet knowing that we have Christ is not so necessary. It is so with a man asleep in a ship: the ship may bring him home safely to the harbor, and yet he may not know it. So Christ may bring us through a sea of boisterous afflictions and temptations to heaven, our haven of rest, and yet we know not of it till we come there.

Fourth, let me tell you this likewise for your comfort: though you do not know that Christ is yours, yet Christ knows that you are His. Will you count your child an unhappy child because he does not know that you are his father? It does not matter if the child does not know that you are his father so long as you know that he is your child. So it is no great matter if you do not know that Christ is yours so long as Christ knows that you are His.

"For the foundation of the Lord standeth sure, the Lord knows who are His." Thus now, beloved, I have done with this use that belongs to this examination, both for those who say they have Christ when they have not, and also for those who say they have not Christ when they have.

4

The Misery of a Man Without Christ

"That at that time ye were without Christ."
Ephesians 2:12

I come now to the third question that I promised to handle, which is to show the misery and sad condition of a man without an interest in Jesus Christ. And, oh, that I could speak it, and have you hear it, with a bleeding heart to see in what a dismal, doleful, and deplorable condition into which every poor soul in the world without Christ is plunged. I shall reduce all that I have to say touching this particular under these two heads, to show you, positively, what he undergoes, and, privatively, what he wants. I shall run over them briefly.

For the positive part, the misery of a man outside of Christ lies in these three great evils under which every man out of Jesus Christ lies:

1. A man out of Christ is surrounded and compassed about with misery whichever way he turns himself. And to illustrate this the more fully, I shall here lay down eight particulars wherein a Christless man is compassed about with miseries on all sides. You are surrounded with misery, O Christless man, if you look either outward or inward, upward or downward, forward or backward, on your right hand or on your left; nothing but miseries accompany you.

If you look outward, all the creatures are armed against you; and hence it is so often expressed in Scripture that the "beast shall be at war with the wicked, but at peace with the godly." All the creatures are against you to avenge their Master's quarrel.

Look within you, and there you shall find a galling, accusing, and condemning conscience, hauling you to the judgment seat and witnessing against you. Your conscience shall be like a thousand witnesses to witness against you and register and enroll all your sins till the day of judgment.

Look upwards into the heavens, and there is nothing but an angry God, a severe judge who has a flame of fire, a furbished sword, and a sharp arrow, and all against you. Romans 1:18: "The wrath of God is revealed from heaven against all ungodliness and unrighteousness of men who hold the truth in unrighteousness."

If you look downwards, there is death ready to receive you, which is but as a back door to let you into hell; and if you look lower, there is nothing but a dungeon of darkness where infernal spirits are reserved in chains of darkness to the judgment of the great day. Whichever way a Christless man looks, there are nothing but miseries accompanying him. If he looks outward, there the creatures are against him; if he looks inward, there is a galled and accusing conscience ready to accuse him; if he looks above him, there is an angry God against him; if he looks below him, there is the devil ready to receive him. A Christless man is in a most sad and doleful condition, as I might exemplify by this familiar similitude: suppose a man were falling into a great and dark dungeon, wherein there were nothing but toads and serpents, and all manner of venomous beasts; and as he is falling in, he catches hold of a twig of a tree that grows over the mouth of the dungeon. And then suppose a lean beast should come and begin to gnaw and bite off that twig. What a miserable case will that poor man be in! Why, just so it is with you, O Christless man: your life is this twig, and death is the lean beast that is biting off this twig of life; and then you fall down into a dungeon of darkness; there is nothing but the twig of life between thee and hell.

If you look before you, there is nothing but misery likewise approaching you; and these are the snares and temptations the devil lays in your way to ensnare you and entice you to sin. There is not a step you tread, nor any company you keep, but the devil lays a trap to ensnare you.

If you look behind you, there is nothing but a huge heap of past sins unrepented of, unsatisfied for, and unpardoned that are able to sink you into the bottomless pit of hell. How, then, can you think of your past sins with anything but a sad heart! How dreadful is it to consider how many thousands of sins you have been guilty of, and yet never have been humbled for them, nor ever shed one penitential tear for them. The guilt of the least of them is enough to plunge you into hell forever.

Look on your right hand, and there are all the blessings of God, all your fullness and prosperity. Your riches and great estate are all made a curse to you. God gives a wicked man riches for his hurt. Ecclesiastes 5:13 tells us that prosperity shall kill the soul of the wicked. O Christless man, your riches and prosperity are all instruments and means to further your everlasting ruin and destruction.

Look on your left hand, and there are all the miseries, afflictions, sufferings, reproaches, diseases, and sad accidents that you meet with as so many forerunners of those unutterable, intolerable, and unsupportable sufferings which a Christless man shall undergo to all eternity.

Oh, then, unhappy man that you are, who does not have an interest in Jesus Christ! Without you and within you, above you and below you, before you and behind you, on your right hand and on your left, there are nothing but miseries accompanying you on every side.

Thus much for the first positive part, of the misery of a Christless man. It is a very sad point that I am now upon, and therefore I shall sweeten all in the close with two or three words of consolation.

2. But, beloved, follow me now. You who are a Christless man or woman, your misery in the positive part of it lies in this: there will be nothing in the world so dismal and intolerable to your soul as the apprehensions of a God without Jesus Christ. God is an amiable, desirable, and universal good in Christ; yet out of Christ, this great

God, who is so good and rich in mercy, and in free grace, is clothed with red and scarlet. You who are out of Christ cannot look upon God but with dreadful apprehensions of Him; you cannot look upon God as a God of mercy to pardon you, but as an angry judge ready to condemn you; not as a friend who seeks your welfare, but as an enemy who sets himself in battle array against you to ruin you. You cannot look upon Him as the rock of ages, in the cliffs whereof you may find safety, but as a burdensome stone, the weight whereof will beat you down and grind you to powder. You cannot look upon God as a refiner's fire to purge away your dross, but as a consuming fire and everlasting burning to consume you to ashes. These are the awakening and soul-frightening apprehensions which every poor soul who does not have an interest in Christ must see; the apprehensions of God will be very dreadful to you.

3. Your misery in the positive part of it, lies in this: that all the creatures and blessings you enjoy in the world are a curse to you, for all blessings are given in and through Christ. There is no blessing given you as a blessing, no mercy given to you as a mercy, if Christ, who is the mercy of all mercies, is not given to you. And here I shall show you your misery in this particular, under these five headings:

First, to have an estate is a blessing of God, but yet all the estate, revenues, and substance which you have gotten by the labor of your hands and the sweat of your brows are all accursed to you if you do not have an interest in Jesus Christ. Deuteronomy 28:16–19: "Cursed shalt thou be in the city, and cursed shalt thou be in the field; cursed shalt be thy basket and thy store; cursed shalt be the fruit of thy body and the fruit of thy land, the increase of thy kind and the flocks of thy sheep; cursed shalt thou be when thou comest in, and cursed shalt thou be when thou goest out." Job 20:15: "He hath swallowed down riches, and he shall vomit them up again." In Ecclesiastes 5:13, Solomon said, "There is a sore evil which I have seen under the sun, namely, riches kept for the owners thereof to their hurt."

Second, you are cursed in your house likewise, as in Job 18:15: "The terrors of God shall dwell in the tabernacles of the wicked," and, "brimstone shall be scattered upon his habitation." And so it is in that place I quoted before, Deuteronomy 28:19

Third, you are cursed in your name. Proverbs 10:17: "The name of the wicked shall rot."

Fourth, you are cursed in your calling. Proverbs 21:4: "The plowing of the wicked is sin." Deuteronomy 28:20: "The Lord shall send upon thee cursing, vexation, and rebuke, in all that thou settest thy hand unto for to do."

Fifth, you are cursed not only in your estate, in your house, in your land, and in your calling, but in your eating and drinking too. You have a strange expression for this in Job 20:23: "When he is about to fill his belly, God shall cast the fury of His wrath upon him, and shall rain it upon him while he is eating." Psalm 78:30–31: "While their meat was yet in their mouths, the wrath of the Lord came upon them."

Thus you see the positive part of man's misery out of Christ, what he undergoes. We come now to show you the privative part of his misery, what he wants; and here much might be said in declaring the misery of a Christless man in the privative part of it, in those things which he lacks in being without an interest in Christ. I shall run over this briefly, and comprise all that I have to say to you under these six headings, and then come to the application.

First, are you without Christ? Why, then, you are without strength. John 15:5: "Without Me ye can do nothing," said Christ. Nay, Paul went further in 2 Corinthians 3:5: "We are of ourselves as of ourselves, says he, not able to think a good thought, but all our sufficiency is from God." Herein lies the misery of a man out of Christ: he is able to do nothing. He is like Samson without his hair: he who before could break iron bands like so many straws, now his strength was no more than another man's. Beloved, you are very weak indeed, if you want Christ. In Isaiah 45:24, it is said that "Christ is made unto a believer, righteousness and strength." Now if you want Christ, you want righteousness by way of acceptance, and you want strength by way of assistance. But to branch this out more particularly, I shall show you in five particulars wherein a man without Jesus Christ wants strength.

• Every man outside of Christ lacks strength to perform any duty. Romans 8:26: "We know not what to pray for, as we ought." We are able to do nothing that is spiritually good of ourselves; all our duties and services, without the righteousness of Christ added to them, are but like so many ciphers. Now, you know, put one thousand ciphers together and they make no sum, but if one figure is prefixed to them, they make an innumerable number. So all our duties, of themselves, are worth nothing, but when Christ is added to them, that puts an estimate upon them, and makes them of considerable value and worth.

• You are without strength to exercise any grace. A dead man is as well able to stir, as a man without Christ is able to take one step heavenward. If God should say, "I will save your soul and give you heaven, could you but perform one duty or exercise one grace," you could not do it, and therefore Christ told us in John 15:5, "Unless you are in Me, you can bring forth no fruit."

• Without Christ, you are without strength to subdue any lust. Oh, how unable are you to keep under a predominant and turbulent lust! Every sin will prevail and domineer in your soul. In Galatians 2:20 Paul says, "I have crucified sin, yet not I, but Christ that liveth in me." The messenger of Satan who was sent to buffet Paul would have prevailed over him if Christ had not helped him. You are not able to subdue any lust without Christ.

• You are without strength to resist any temptation. In Ephesians 6:10, Paul exhorts them there to be "strong in the Lord and in the power of His might"; not in the power of *their* might, for they were not able to stand of themselves by their own strength, but be strong in the Lord, and in the power of *His* might. So when David came to fight against great Goliath, had he gone out to meet him in his own strength he would have been overcome and devoured; but he went against him in the name, and in the strength of the Lord of hosts.

• A man without Christ is without strength to bear or undergo any afflictions. Every affliction that is but like a feather to one who is in Christ will be like a lump of lead. A godly man, if he has in any way withdrawn himself from Christ's aid and assistance, a little affliction will sink him, for it is given us of God not only to do, but to suffer for His sake (see Philippians 1:29), intimating that unless God enables us to suffer, we are not able to bear up our spirits under any affliction.

Thus, then, you see that if you want an interest in Christ, you want strength in these five particulars to perform any duty, to exercise any grace, to subdue any lust, to resist any temptation, or to bear any affliction.

If you are without Christ, you are not only without strength, but without growth likewise. Jesus Christ is to the souls of men what the warm beams of the sun are to the earth: take away the influence of the warm beams of the sun from the earth and all the grass of the field, and every herb and green thing will die and wither away presently. So Christ is our Sun of righteousness: take away Christ from a man and there will be no blossoms of grace budding forth in that man's heart. Adam's stock is a barren root upon which no branch of grace will spring forth. You can never bring forth any fruit unto God unless you are grafted not upon Adam's stock, but upon the stock of the root of Jesse. A man, during his unconverted state, is the devil's slave, and he never brings forth fruit till he comes to be in Christ. Only in and through Christ are we enabled to bring forth acceptable fruit unto God.

Without Christ you are likewise without worth. Though you are the son of a noble, and of the offspring of princes, though you can lay claim to thousands and thousands per annum, yet without Christ you are poor, wretched, miserable, blind, and naked, Revelation 3:17. For it is Christ alone who is the repository and storehouse of all wisdom and knowledge, and all the treasures of it are bound up in Him.

Without Christ you are without comfort. This is a deplorable misery; a man without Christ is without comfort. As that would be an uncomfortable dwelling where the sun did not shine by day, nor the moon by night, even so would your soul be very disconsolate if Christ did not shine on your heart. The comforts of a child of God either ebb or flow as Christ either comes *to* him or goes *from* him.

Without Christ you are without liberty. If the Son makes you free, then you are free indeed, John 8:36. And unless the Son makes you free, you are slaves indeed— slaves to sin, slaves to your lusts, slaves to the creatures, and slaves to the devil by whom you are taken captive at his will. You are never free men and women till the Son makes you free.

If you are without Jesus Christ, you are without beauty. You are only like a carcass without life or a body without a head. It is Christ only who gives us beauty and comeliness. Ezekiel 16:14: "And thy renown went forth among the heathen for thy beauty, for it was perfect through my comeliness which I had put upon thee, saith the Lord God." If we do not have the comeliness of Christ upon us, we are not comely. You have a pretty passage in Luke 2:32. Christ is there called the glory of the children of Israel. Christ is the glory of the children of Israel who believe in Him. There is no glory, but a body full of sores and botches in all those who are out of Christ.

Application

And thus now, beloved, I am done with the doctrinal part of this point, that every man, during the state of his unregeneracy, is without any actual interest in Christ. We come now to the application, and here I might say to you, as a learned author was wont to say when he had been handling any terrible subject, and treating upon doctrines of terror, he would always say, "O godly man, this belongs not to you." So may I say to you, "O godly soul, this pertains not to you. The misery and sad condition of a man out of Christ belongs not to you." You do not now hear

the sentence which shall be passed upon you, but you now
hear the misery that you are freed and redeemed from.

USE OF CONSOLATION. May the Lord uphold and
comfort the hearts of all you who can lay a just claim to
Jesus Christ.

Happy, oh, three times happy are you, that ever you
were born who have an interest in Jesus Christ; for though
God is clothed with majesty, great and terrible in Himself,
yet you can look upon Him under apprehensions of love,
mercy, peace, goodness, tenderness, and kindness. You
are to look upon God not as an angry judge to condemn
you, but as a Father of mercy to comfort you; not as an ad-
versary in battle array against you, but as a friend reconciled to you; not as a burdensome stone that may grind
you to powder, but as the Rock of Ages, in the cliffs
whereof you may find safety. You are to look upon God
not as a consuming fire to burn you, but as a refiner's fire
to purge away your dross, sin, and corruption. It is Christ's
blood alone that quenches the fire of God's anger. So now
you may look upon God under all these apprehensions of
love, mercy, peace, pardon, and reconciliation if you have
an interest in Jesus Christ.

Happy, yea, three times happy are you in having an interest in Christ, for though you have nothing here in the
world, yet you have all things. You have all things by having an interest in Christ, who has all things. You may say,
as Paul said of himself in 2 Corinthians 6:10: "As having
nothing, and yet possessing all things." Though you want
many things here below, yet if you have an interest in
Christ you have all things. It may be you eat of the bread
of affliction and drink of the water of adversity, yet happy
are you if, with all, you can but drink drafts of Christ's
blood, if Christ bids you eat of His body and drink of his
blood. Song of Solomon 5:1: "Eat O friends, drink, yea,
drink abundantly, O my beloved." Happy are you who are
clothed with the long white robes of Christ's righteousness. Though you have nothing here below, yet you have
all things by having Christ, who has all things. 1 Corinthians 3:22–23: "All are yours, and ye are Christ's."

OBJECTION. But here some may object and say, "How can this be? How can it be said that a believer has all things, when many times he has the *least* of the things of this world?
ANSWER. A believer may be said to have all things in these four ways:
He has all things equivalently.
He has all things conditionally.
He has all things finally.
And he has all things inheritavely, or by inheritance.
A believer has all things equivalently, that is, in having Christ he has as good as if he had all things. He has that which is of more worth than if he had all the world. That man is not accounted a rich man who has much lumber and household stuff in his house, but he who has many jewels in his cabinet. Now Christ is the pearl of great price, the jewel of all jewels. In having Christ you have all things; you have that which is more worth than all things.
A believer has all things conditionally. If such a thing is for your good which you desire, you shall have it, be it what it will be. Psalm 84:11: "The Lord will give grace and glory, and no good thing will He withhold from those that walk uprightly." He has all things conditionally.
A believer has everything finally, that is, the Lord intended that every creature that He made might be for his use: the sun, moon, stars, and all the other creatures were made for them; nay, and all the angels in heaven were made to be ministering spirits to the heirs of salvation.
All things are a believer's inheritavely, by way of right and inheritance. Though he may not have all things in possession, yet he has all things by way of reversion; he has a right and claim to everything. Psalm 37:11: "The meek shall inherit the earth."
But it now may be I speak to many a poor godly man or woman, and tell them all is theirs, when it may be they have not a penny to buy bread to put in their bellies. Why yet, beloved, let me tell you, though you have nothing, yet you have Christ who is worth all things; though you want other things, yet you do not want Christ. Beloved, you may

want outward blessings and yet not want Jesus Christ; you may want food to put in your mouths and yet not want the bread of life, the Lord Jesus Christ to feed upon; you may want clothes to cover your nakedness, and yet not want the long robes of Christ's righteousness to cover your sinful nakedness; you may want friends to comfort, help, and relieve you, and yet not want Christ to be your Friend.

There is something yet by way of consolation, but I must defer that till another opportunity.

5

The Benefits of Being In Christ

"That at that time ye were without Christ."
Ephesians 2:12

We come now to lay down some other things, by way of comfort, to those who have an interest in Christ. And oh, that you who are citizens of heaven would read over the large charter of mercies that is sealed to you in the blood of Christ! Read over those many benefits and comforts you have by Christ that none in the world enjoy but you who have an interest in Him. I shall reduce all that I have to say concerning this particular under these seven headings, and you who lay an undoubted claim to Christ may lay claim to this sevenfold benefit by Him:

1. You who have an interest in Christ have all things, though you have nothing. This I touched upon before. You may say with the apostle, "As having nothing, yet possessing all things." Though you may be without wealth and riches and olive yards, yet herein lies your comfort: you are not without Christ. In having Him you have all things, though you have nothing, for all things are given you in and through Christ by way of entail. 1 Corinthians 3:22: "All things are yours, and ye are Christ's."

I shall a little explain this place to you. The apostle said, "Whether Paul or Apollos, or Cephas, or the world, or life, or death, or things present, or things to come; all are yours, and ye are Christ's, and Christ is God's." Whether Paul or Apollos or Cephas—that is, all the ministers of Christ—if you have an interest in Christ, Christ has given gifts to his ministers, so Paul is yours and Apollos is yours. They are yours because they are your lights, to guide you in the way to heaven through the dark wilder-

ness of this world; they are your pastors, to feed you with
knowledge and understanding in the mysteries of salvation; they are your shepherds, to gather you into the fold
of Jesus Christ; they are your builders, to hew and square
and make you fit for Christ's spiritual building; they are
your contractors or the friend of the Bridegroom, to make
up a complete match between Christ and you (I speak
only in Scripture phrase); they are your vinedressers, to
prune you and make you fit to bring forth fruit unto God.
Thus all the gifts of all the ministers in the world are intended by Christ for the good of His children. If there
were no godly men in the world, there would be no ministers in the world; and therefore those people who will
hear only one kind of minister, such as they affect and
slight all else, limit their own privileges, for all the ministers in the world are given by Christ for the benefit of His
children.

But then again, says the apostle, "Whether Paul, or
Apollos, or Cephas, or the world, all is yours." You have a
right to all the world, not only a civil right, but a religious
right: "The meek shall inherit the earth." So that if you
could go to the top of an exceedingly high mountain, and
look over all the whole world, you may say, "Behold, I see
all this is my Father's ground, and He has given it to
Christ, even the heathen for His inheritance, and the ut-
termost parts of the earth for His possession, and I, having
an interest in Christ, am thereby a co-heir and joint heir
with Him."

Life is yours. God has given you your lives that, in that
little space of time, you might provide for eternity and labor to know God and worship Him aright.

Death is yours. Death is but, as it were, a launching of
you forth into an ocean of endless joys and pleasures; it is
but a trap door to let you into heaven. If you should never
die, you would be but miserable creatures; but God has
appointed death to be a means to let you into heaven.
"Whether we live, we live unto the Lord, or whether we
die, we die unto the Lord, so that living or dying, we are
the Lord's."

Things present are yours, which includes both present mercies and present afflictions. Present mercies are yours as having a right to them, beholding the goodness of God in them, praising God for them, serving God with them, and doing good to others by them. Present afflictions are yours, likewise, to humble your hearts, to wean you from the world, to quicken your desires after heaven, to purge out your corruptions, and exercise your graces and the like. Whatever present condition you are in, that present condition, be it what it will be, shall work for your good.

Things to come are yours too. If afflictions, or temptations, or troubles, or wants, or famine, or pestilence, or imprisonments, or anything comes, they are all yours. Heaven and happiness, glory, life, and salvation are all yours. Here, then beloved, you see the first branch of a man's happiness who has an interest in Christ. In having Christ he has all things, though he has nothing, because he has Him who has all things.

2. The man who has an interest in Christ, his second consolation lies in this: all that Christ has is his. And, oh, my beloved, this is a gold mine that will afford you many precious comforts. I shall give them to you under these six particulars:

If you have an interest in Christ, then Christ's Father is your Father.

Christ's Spirit is your Spirit.

Christ's righteousness is your righteousness.

Christ's graces are your graces.

Christ's peace is your peace.

And Christ's sufferings are your sufferings.

And, oh, beloved, see what a large field you may here walk in: If you have an interest in Christ, His Father is your Father. In John 20:17 Christ said, "Behold, I ascend unto My Father and your Father, to My God and your God." Christ's Father is a believer's Father.

Christ's Spirit is your Spirit. In John 14:16–17 Christ said, "I will pray to the Father, and He shall give you another Comforter, that He may abide with you forever, even the Spirit of truth, whom the world cannot receive,

because it seeth Him not, neither knoweth Him; but ye
know Him, for He dwelleth with you and shall be in you."

Christ's righteousness is your righteousness. Jeremiah
23:6: "And this is His name whereby He shall be called,
The Lord our righteousness." So we read in 1 Corinthians
1:30: "Christ is made of God unto us wisdom, righteousness, sanctification and redemption."

His graces are your graces. John 1:14: "Christ is full of
grace and truth." Why? That out of His fullness we might
all receive grace for grace, that is, forever grace that is in
Jesus Christ, according to our proportion and capacity, we
shall receive from Him.

Christ's peace is yours. John 14:27: "Peace I leave with
you; My peace I give unto you." The peace we enjoy is
from Christ.

Last, Christ's sufferings are your sufferings. God looks
upon His sufferings for you as if you, in your own persons,
had done and suffered what He did. The just has suffered
for the unjust to bring you to God. The sufferings of
Christ as effectually bring you to God as if you, in your
own persons, had suffered upon the cross as He did. Nay,
it does it a great deal more, for our sufferings could not
have done it. Thus, having an interest in Christ, all that
Christ has is yours.

3. Take this for your comfort: all that you have is
Christ's. I shall sum up all that I have to say concerning
this under these three comprehensive particulars:

Your sins are Christ's, to pardon and satisfy God's justice for them. Your sufferings are Christ's, to sanctify
them. And your bodies and souls are Christ's, to save
them.

You who have an interest in Christ, your sins are His to
pardon. Isaiah 53:6: "The Lord hath laid on Him the iniquity of us all. . . .The chastisement of our peace was laid
upon Him, and with His stripes we are healed." He bore
our sins in His body on the tree, and to this purpose the
apostle has an expression in 2 Corinthians 5:21: "He hath
made Him to be sin for us, that we might be made the
righteousness of God in Him." Christ was no sinner, but

He was made a sinner for us. He bore our sins upon Him; therefore, our sins are Christ's to pardon.

Our sufferings are Christ's sufferings, to sanctify them unto us. In Acts 9:4, Christ said to Saul, "Saul, why persecutest thou Me?" He looked upon the injuries and wrongs done to His people as if they were done to Him.

Your bodies and souls are Christ's to save. Our members are members of Christ's body. In 1 Corinthians 6:15 the apostle said, "Shall I then take the members of Christ, and make them members of a harlot?" God forbid! Your body is Christ's, and your soul is Christ's. The apostle has it in so many expressed terms. 1 Corinthians 6:19–20: "What? Know ye not that your body is the temple of the Holy Ghost, which is in you, which ye have of God, and ye are not your own? For ye are bought with a price; therefore glorify God in your bodies and spirit, which are God's."

Thus you see what a large field of mercy all you who have an interest in Christ have here to walk in. You have all things, though you have nothing: all things equivalently, all things conditionally, all things finally, and all things inheritively. All the ministers of Christ are yours; the whole world is yours; life and death is yours; things present are yours, whether present afflictions or present mercies; things to come are yours, whether afflictions or temptations or trouble or want or anything; mercy to come is yours, life and salvation, heaven and happiness. All is yours: all that Christ has is yours. Christ's Father is your Father; His Spirit is your Spirit; His righteousness is your righteousness; His graces are your graces; His peace is your peace; and His sufferings are your sufferings. And all that you have is Christ's: your sins are Christ's to pardon; your sufferings are Christ's to sanctify; and your souls and bodies are Christ's to save.

I might here add one heading more: all your duties and services are Christ's too. He perfumes them with the sweet odor of His merits, and so presents and makes them acceptable to God. Hence it is that you read in Revelation that Christ adds His incense to the prayers of all His saints; and this is a very great consolation.

4. All you who have an interest in Christ, take this for your comfort: having Christ is that which will sweeten all the crosses and afflictions and adverse conditions that you meet with here in this world. Having Christ will sweeten every trouble. As I told you before, what the tree was to the waters of Marah, that Christ will be to every sad and dejected soul in every troublesome condition. The waters of Marah were so exceedingly bitter that none could drink of them, but when the tree was cast into the waters, they became sweet. Why, your condition here in this world may be as the waters of Marah, full of bitterness and sorrow and trouble and affliction, but now, cast this tree of life, the Lord Jesus, into these waters and this will convert them from waters of Marah, bitter and troublesome, into rivers of joy and streams of comfort. Christ will be to your soul as the honey in the lion's belly was to Samson: it became good for food to feed upon. Afflictions and troubles may come in upon you like a roaring lion, but Christ is as the honey in this lion that sweetens all your sorrows, and makes them advantageous and comfortable for you.

I might apply to this purpose what an author observed concerning the water of the sea: it has salt in it, but when it runs through the bowels of the earth it loses its saltiness and becomes pleasant. So, though your condition in the world is full of sharp and sore afflictions, yet, when these come to run through Christ, He sweetens them all unto you. Great is your comfort in having an interest in Christ, for this is that which sweetens all the crosses and troubles you meet with here in the world. And, beloved, seriously consider it, and let me a little reason the case with you. What if you feed on the bread of sorrow, yet how can you be uncomfortable when with all that you feed upon the bread of life, the Lord Jesus Christ? What if you drink the water of affliction and wine of astonishment, yet how can you be uncomfortable as long as you drink drops of Christ's blood? What if you have no house to put your head in, let this be your comfort: you have a house reserved for you, a building not made with hands, eternal in the heavens. What if you have nothing but a stone for your pillow to lay your head upon, when every night you lay your head in the bosom of Jesus Christ? This much concerning the fourth consolation.

5. All you who have a real and well-grounded interest in Christ, herein lies your comfort: in and through Christ you may look upon God (who in Himself is clothed with dread and terribleness) with a great deal of joy and comfort. Christ makes all the attributes of God to be delightful and comfortable to you. Though God is a consuming fire to burn up your soul like stubble, if you are out of Christ, yet *in* Christ you may look upon God as fire, but yet so as that Christ interposes between you and the fire. Christ is as a screen between the fire of God's wrath and you. You are to look upon God not as an enemy who sets Himself against you, but as a friend reconciled to you; not as an angry judge who desires to condemn you, but as a merciful Father who is willing to pardon you. You are not to look upon God as being clothed with dread and terror, but with mercy and compassion. God will frown upon you out of Christ, but bring Christ in your arms, and present Him to God the Father, and then He will turn away His anger from you and behold you with a smiling countenance. If you are in Christ and Christ is in you, and God is well pleased with His Son, He must be well pleased with you too. Great is your benefit by having an interest in Christ. I may say in this case what Elisha the prophet said to King Jeroboam in 2 Kings 3:14: "Surely, says he, ere it not that I regard the presence of Jehoshaphat king of Judah, I would not look toward thee nor see thee." Just so does God say to us, "Were it not for My Son Jesus Christ, you would never see My face, nor have a good look from Me."

6. If you have a real interest in Christ, then this is another part of your comfort: God the Father as truly accepts you in His Son as if you had, in your own person, done and suffered what Christ did. This is a great benefit. God accepts what Christ has done for us as if we had done it ourselves. Ephesians 1:6: "He hath made us accepted in

the Beloved," that is, in Christ. God looks upon you in Christ, and accepts all your duties and performances as well as if you had prayed as well as ever Christ prayed, and done and suffered as much as ever Christ did.

7. Are you now in Christ? Well take this for your comfort: you may be confidently assured that you shall be one day with Christ. This is the last consolation, and I shall give you a pregnant text to prove it, though it is not so well understood in the common reading of it as it should be. Romans 8:10: "If Christ be in you, the body is dead because of sin, but the Spirit is life because of righteousness." What is the meaning of this, that the body is dead because of sin? The meaning is not that the body does not mortify sin, but the body is dead because of sin, that is, sin shall bring your bodies to the grave, but your spirits shall live because of righteousness, that is, the righteousness of Jesus Christ. Through the righteousness of Christ, your souls shall live forever in glory with Christ. Though your bodies die, and sin brings them to the grave, yet the killing of your bodies shall but make way for the living of your spirits. Being in Christ here, you shall forever live with Christ in glory hereafter. The death of your bodies shall but give you an entrance into glory, and therefore why should death be grievous to those who are in Christ Jesus? For death is but, as it were, the marriage day wherein Christ and their souls shall be united together.

If Christ is in you, your bodies shall die because of sin, but your spirits shall live because of righteousness. You have another pertinent place to prove this in John 17:23–24. Christ said there, "I in them, and Thou in Me, that they may be made perfect in one, and that the world may know that Thou hast sent Me, and hast loved them as Thou hast loved Me; and Father I will that they also whom Thou hast given Me be with Me where I am, that they may behold My glory which Thou hast given Me." Some conceive that this prayer of Christ was made only for the apostles, that they might be where Christ was in heaven, but if you mark the preceding words you shall find that it was for all believers, for says Christ himself, "Neither pray I for these alone, but for all those that shall believe in Me through their word." Great is your comfort in having an interest in Christ here; you shall one day reign with Him forever in glory.

Thus I have done with these seven consolations to those who have a real and well grounded interest in Christ. I have only now a word or two, by way of use, to apply and set home what I have said concerning this particular. Here you see what unspeakable comforts redound to you who have nothing. Christ is yours, and all that Christ has is yours, and all that you have is Christ's. Christ sweetens all afflictions and crosses to you, and having Christ represents God the Father to you, not with terror and dread, but with goodness, meekness, loving-kindness, mercy, and long-suffering. Through Christ, God as freely accepts you and what you do as if it were done as well as ever Christ did it. Being in Christ here, you shall forever live with Christ in glory hereafter. Oh, how should all these mercies and privileges stir up all those who have yet no part in Christ, never to give rest to their eyes, nor slumber to their eyelids, till they have gotten an interest in Him.

6

Characteristics of Having an Interest in Christ

"That at that time ye were without Christ."
Ephesians 2:12

Lest any of you who hear me this day should lie under a spirit of delusion, and think that all that I have said touching the happiness of those who have an interest in Christ belongs to them when it does not, I shall therefore spend this hour in showing you some characters whereby you may know whether you have a real interest in Christ or not. This is the most needful point that ever in my life I pressed upon you, and may the Lord give you grace to lay these characters close to your own hearts, and by them seriously to examine your own souls whether you have a real interest in Christ or not. But before I give you these characters, give me leave to premise these cautions, which will the better make way to handling the point in hand.

CAUTION 1. Men may be strongly conceited and opinionated that they have an interest in Christ when they have not. I shall give you a plain text for this in 2 Corinthians 10:7: "Do ye look on things after the outward appearance? If any man trust to himself that he is Christ's, let him of himself think this again, that as he is Christ's, even so are we Christ's." This is a very notable place; there were some among the Corinthians who strongly believed they belonged to Christ when they did not. Also, they had an ill opinion of the apostles, and thought they did *not* belong to Christ. To such as these the apostle Paul here speaks. Men may strongly believe they have an interest in Christ when there is no such matter. So it was with the church of Laodicea. Revelation 3:17: "Thou sayest I am rich and increased with goods, and have need of nothing; and knowest not that thou art wretched, and miserable, and poor, and blind, and naked."

CAUTION 2. I would have you take notice of laying down the characters of a man who has an interest in Christ. I do not so press them that, unless you have them all in you, you cannot have an interest in Christ, for if you have but one of them in you, in truth and sincerity, it is an evidence that you have an interest in Christ. Rather, I give you this caution for fear of casting down any poor dejected soul. If you have but one link of this golden chain, you have as sure hold as if you had all of it.

CAUTION 3. In laying down these characters of one who has an interest in Christ, I lay them down only in the affirmative, not in the negative; that is, all those who have these characters in them may be confidently assured that they have an interest in Christ. But I do not say that those who do not have these characters in them do not have an interest in Christ. This I say that you may confidently and indubitably know and be assured that you have an interest in Christ, if you find these things in you.

CAUTION 4. Last, take in this caution likewise, that in giving you these characters I shall not press them so as if to say that having all these in exercise and feeling and in your own apprehensions can only evidence your having an interest in Christ; but if you have them in habit and in truth, though not in exercise and practice, it is sufficient to evidence your interest in Christ. For a poor soul may have many graces of God's Spirit in truth in him, though he does not feel and exercise and apprehend them in himself. I told you it was so with Mary Magdalene: she talked to Christ face to face and said, "They have taken away my Lord, and I know not where they have laid Him." And thus I have done with the cautions wherein I have only made way for my better proceeding in giving you the several characters of a man who has a real interest in Christ. And I wish to God they may be all engraven upon every one of your hearts, so that you may be unquestionably assured in your own souls of your interest in Him. I shall reduce all I have to say concerning this particular under eleven headings:

1. The man who has an interest in Christ is cast out of himself, that is, he is cast out of all conceit of his own self-sufficiency and righteousness, good works or merits. No man is in Christ but he is out of himself. This character the apostle gives you in Philippians 3:8–9: "Yea, doubtless, I count all things but loss for the excellency of the knowledge of Christ Jesus my Lord, for whom I have suffered the loss of all things, and do count them but dung, that I may win Christ, and be found in Him, not having mine own righteousness." Here Paul, having won Christ, would not be found having his own righteousness. The apostle does not mean his own righteousness in point of being, but in point of dependence: not having his own righteousness so as to be justified by it. In that regard he would not be found having it. So in 1 Corinthians 4:4 the apostle says, "I know nothing by myself." Now one would think this man a very holy and exact man, for, says he, "I know nothing by myself," that is, I know no sin upon my soul that I perform wittingly or willingly. But mark the next words, "yet am I not hereby justified." He was quite out of conceit of all the good works that ever he did. Every man who is in Christ is out of himself: he sees his own *in*sufficiency and Christ's *all*-sufficiency; he sees his emptiness of grace and Christ's fullness of grace; he sees himself to be nothing and Christ to be all in all. In Luke 16:15 Christ said to the Pharisees: "Ye are they which justify yourselves before men, but God knoweth your hearts." It is as if He had said, "You think well of yourselves and your graces, but God knows your hearts, that you are not such as you seem to be."

And therefore, beloved, consider seriously, if God has wrought this grace in your hearts so that you are cast out of yourselves to see your own emptiness, vileness, insufficiency, and want of Christ; if there is this work of grace wrought in you—then you may know you have a real part and portion in Jesus Christ.

2. A man in Christ makes conscience of keeping every

known command of Christ. This you have in 1 John 2:5: "Whoso keepeth His Word, in him verily is the love of God perfected; hereby know we that we are in Him." Hereby we know that we are in Christ, if we keep every known command of Christ. And therefore you who can appeal to heaven that there is no one command of Christ but bears sway in your heart, and carries an authority over your conscience so that you can subject yourselves to it, although you have many weaknesses and failings, yet this is an undoubted character that you are in Christ. 1 John 2:24: "If that which ye have heard from the beginning shall remain in you, you also shall continue in the Son and in the Father." You who keep every known command of Christ have an interest in Him and He in you. And therefore, beloved, all you who make conscience of keeping the known and revealed will of God, so that there is no known sin but you labor to avoid, and no known grace but you labor to exercise, and no known duty but you labor to perform, if it is thus with you, you may comfort yourselves that you have a real interest in Christ.

3. He who has an interest in Christ has a power derived from Christ, enabling him to mortify his inward and bosom lusts. Galatians 5:24: "They that are Christ's have crucified the flesh with the affections and lusts." When Christ came in the flesh among us, we crucified Him, but if ever Christ comes in your heart, He will crucify you. The crucifying of the flesh with the affections and lusts that the apostle here speaks of is not the killing and total extirpation of sin, but giving a deadly blow to sin so that sin shall never reign in us, nor have dominion over us any more. If you are in Christ, sin will be like those beasts spoken of in Daniel: their dominion was taken away, but their lives were preserved for a little season. So the dominion of sin will be taken away. Sin shall not reign in you, yet the life and being of sin will remain in you for a little season. But still, as the house of Saul grew weaker and weaker while the house of David grew stronger and stronger, so if Christ dwells in your heart, sin in your soul will every day grow weaker and weaker, and grace in your heart will

grow stronger and stronger. And therefore, beloved, all you whose hearts can bear you witness that you have had the power of mortifying grace upon your souls, that you can bridle your beloved lusts, subdue your bosom sins, and curb the pride of your hearts, you may then lay an undoubted claim to Jesus Christ.

4. The man who has an interest in Christ keeps a strict watch over his own heart. He will not wittingly or willingly give way to the least sin to dishonor God. A man in Christ keeps a watchful eye over himself so that He does not give way to the least sin to dishonor Jesus Christ. "We know that whosoever is born of God sinneth not, but he that is begotten of God keepeth himself, and that wicked one toucheth him not." He who is begotten of God keeps himself; he does not keep himself from all sin, but as much as in him lies he resists every sin and temptation; he keeps himself from every known sin. 1 John 3:6: "Whosoever abideth in Him sinneth not." This is not spoken absolutely, but comparatively: he sins not in comparison of those great sins that wicked men commit, for they are slaves to their lusts. Second, he sins not, that is deliberately—neither with a delightful complacency, nor with a total obduracy, nor in a way of final impenitency. In these regards a man in Christ sins not.

And now, beloved, you whose hearts and consciences can bear you witness that you keep a strict watch over your own souls, and that you have a care of committing the least sin against God whereby you might dishonor Him, if it is thus with you, you have an infallible evidence of your interest in Christ. The man who keeps sin *out* of his heart may be confidently assured that he has Christ *in* his heart.

5. That man has an interest in Christ Jesus in whom Christ has wrought a real change, both in his life and nature. If you are in Christ, He will be in you to work an effectual and saving change, both in your heart and life. In 2 Corinthians 5:17 the apostle says, "If any man be in Christ, he is a new creature; old things are passed away, behold all things are become new." Why now, beloved, take this text and lay it close to your hearts. Has God

made you new creatures, and wrought a saving change in your heart? Can you evidence to your own souls that ever since you were first born, you were new born? If it is so, you may lay a confident claim to Jesus Christ. If any man is in Christ, he is a new creature.

6. The man who has an interest in Christ grows up in Christ to be fruitful in every good work. Hence it is that you often read in the Scripture of growing up in Christ, and increasing in Christ with the increase of God. Jesus Christ is the root of Jesse, in whom, whoever is rooted and ingrafted, He will bring forth fruit unto God. Whoever is engrafted into Christ will bring forth the fruits of righteousness to the praise and glory of God. John 15:5: "I am the vine (says Christ) and ye are the branches; he that abideth in Me and I in him, the same bringeth forth much fruit; for without Me you can do nothing." Now, beloved, you who make it out to your own souls that you grow in grace, knowledge, understanding, and in the duties of sanctification, humiliation, and mortification, this is a sure argument that you are planted into that root of Jesse that makes you to bring forth fruit unto God.

7. The man who has an interest in Christ is most humble and vile in his own eyes. Of all the men in the world, there is no man so debased in his own esteem as he who has an interest in Christ. Mark Paul's description of a man in Christ in 2 Corinthians 12:2–5: "I knew a man in Christ above fourteen years ago, whether in the body or out of the body, I cannot tell, God knoweth, such a man caught up into paradise, and heard unspeakable things, which is not lawful for a man to utter. Of such a one will I glory, yet of myself I will not glory, but in my infirmities." Here Paul says of himself that he would not boast of what good either he had or did, or of what glory he beheld, lest men should think of him above that which is meet. This is the badge of a man in Christ: he is most humble in his own eyes. Those vessels that are most full make the least sound, whereas those that are empty make the greatest noise. So those Christians who are full of grace and have Christ dwelling in them walk most humbly and make the least

noise, while those who are out of Christ, and empty of all grace and goodness, keep the greatest boasting of all. As shallow rivers make the greatest noise in running over the pebblestones, while the deeper streams glide away silently, so shallow brains, who know very little or nothing as they ought to know, make the greatest show of what they seem to have, while others who know more and are deeper learned are silent.

It is very remarkable what one observed concerning the prophet Ezekiel. He was a very holy man, and much conversant with visions and revelations, yet this man who was full of so many admirable parts, gifts, and graces, the Holy Ghost no less than ninety-three times in that prophecy calls by the name of the Son of Man, which was (said he) to keep him humble, abate pride in his heart, and show that where there is most of Christ and grace in the heart, that man should be most humble and vile in his own eyes.

8. A man in Christ will take care and make conscience of walking worthy of his interest in Christ. The apostle gives a caution for this in Colossians 2:6–7: "As ye have therefore received Christ Jesus the Lord, so walk ye in Him, rooted and built up in Him," that is, according to those beginnings you have made, and those gospel-discoveries God has given you, and that entertainment you have already given to Christ Jesus the Lord, so now it becomes you to make a suitable progress. As truly and really and purely as you have received Him; so let it be your everyday work to be making progress in Him, and to walk worthy of Him. So in 1 John 2:6, "He that saith he abideth in Him, ought himself also so to walk, even as He walked." Hence it is that you find in Scripture that being in Christ and living a godly life are both joined together. And 2 Timothy 3:12: "All that will live godly in Christ Jesus." That man whose person is in Christ will labor that his ways may be in Christ too. Many a one would gladly have his *person* in Christ, though his *life* is not in Christ; but those whose persons and ways are both in Christ may lay a comfortable claim to Him.

The difference between a man who has an interest in Christ and one who has none I shall demonstrate to you by this familiar example. A man who by experience knows what it is to clean a room will be careful that he does not, upon every slight occasion, dirty it again, because he knows what pains and labor are taken to clean it. But a dog comes in and never cares for dirtying it because he does not know what it takes to make it clean. So it is that a godly man will be careful of walking worthy of his interest in Christ because he knows how much it cost him—how many tears, sighs, groans, and prayers before he got an interest in Christ, and an assurance of His love. But a wicked man makes no conscience of sinning against Christ and displeasing Him, because he never knew what it was to get an interest in Him. In Galatians 3:27 the apostle says, "As many as have Christ, they have put on Christ." A very learned interpreter had an exceedingly good note upon this text. He said that this speech of the apostle here is an allusion to an ancient custom among the heathens, that when they came to the profession of the faith they were wont always, between Easter and Whitsuntide, to put off their old garments and put on white raiments. The end of it was to typify and note that once they were in Christ they must leave their old courses and conversations and now labor to walk after a more holy, blameless, and innocent life in their carriage towards God. Thus, beloved, if you have an interest in Christ, you have put on Christ, walking worthy of Him in a holy, pure, spotless, and unblameable life and conversation.

9. A man who has an interest in Christ so prizes Him that he would not be without Him for all the world. There is no man who is in Christ but looks upon Him as the most amiable and desirable good in the world. He knows the worth of Christ, and counts Him as an invaluable treasure. In 1 Peter 2:7, the apostle, after he had told them of their being built upon Christ, as lively stones upon the foundation, concludes, "unto you therefore which believe, Christ is precious," intimating that whoever is founded and bottomed upon Christ, Christ is very pre-

cious to that soul. And therefore you, beloved, who have a
sure testimony in your own consciences that you set a high
price and value and esteem upon Christ above all things
in the world, and that you count all other things as dross
and dung in comparison to an interest in Christ, this is a
very good and undoubted evidence that you have an interest in Him. It was an excellent speech of one, concerning his interest in Christ: "If all the stones in my house
were diamonds, and all the dust in my house shavings of
gold, and every pebble stone an orient pearl, yet would I
not prize nor value these in comparison of my interest in
Christ."

10. He who has an interest in Christ has the Spirit of
Christ dwelling in His soul. 1 John 4:13: "Hereby know we
that we dwell in Him, and He in us, because He hath
given us of His Spirit." He conveys His Spirit, through the
golden conduit pipes of His ordinances, into your heart.
This is a sure evidence to you of your interest in Christ, if
you have the Spirit of Christ dwelling in you in this threefold operation of it: if you have the enlightening work of
the Spirit to enlighten your mind to know Christ; if you
have the inclining work of the Spirit to incline your heart
to love Christ; and if you have the enforcing operation of
the Spirit to empower your wills to obey Christ. If you enjoy the Spirit of God in these three operations of it, then
you may certainly know that you have an interest in Christ.

11. He who has an interest in Christ labors by all possible means to bring others to the knowledge of Christ.
Paul, before he was in Christ, labored to drive men from
Christ, but afterwards, when he was converted, he labored
to draw men to Christ more abundantly than all the rest
of the apostles. Oh, beloved, you who can show compassion to poor souls in their natural condition, and can
heartily wish all men to be in Christ as well as yourselves,
you who can bemoan the Christless condition of your
friends and neighbors, this is a very evident discovery of
your interest in Christ.

Thus I have done with these several characteristics of a
man who is in Christ. If you are cast out of yourself, and

out of an opinion of your own goodness and righteousness; if you make conscience of keeping every known command of Christ, and have a power derived from Christ, enabling you to mortify your bosom and inward lusts; if you have a care to avoid every sin whereby you might dishonor Christ; if there is a real change wrought in you, both in heart and life, from nature to grace; if you grow up in Christ to be fruitful in every good work, and are humble and base and vile in your own eyes; if you labor to walk worthy of your interest in Christ, prizing and valuing Him above all the desirable things of the world; if the Spirit of Christ dwells in you, enlightening your minds to know Him, inclining your hearts to love Him, and empowering your wills to obey Him: and, last, if you have ardent desires and earnest endeavors to win others to Christ as well as yourselves; if you can find any one of these in truth and sincerity in your hearts, it will be a very good evidence to you of your interest in Christ.

I have only a word or two more to those who, upon examination, really find themselves to be in a condition without Jesus Christ. Let me leave with you these three discoveries of your sad condition, to quicken you the more earnestly in your pursuits after Him.

Are you without Christ? Then you are without satisfaction and contestation in all the things you enjoy here in this world. What Solomon says is verified in you, that "your eye shall not be satisfied with seeing, nor your ear with hearing." Nothing without Jesus Christ can give satisfaction to the demands of an immortal soul. The world is round and your hearts are triangular; and you know it is impossible that a round thing should fill that which is three square. So neither is it possible that the world, or anything in it, should satisfy the desires of your hearts.

As you can have no satisfaction in the world, so neither can you have any acceptance with God. God will say to you, as Joseph did to his brethren, "If you bring not up your brother Benjamin with you, look me not in the face." So will God say to you, "If you bring not Jesus Christ your elder brother with you, do not look Me in the face." Here is the misery of a Christless man: he can have no acceptance with God.

Without an interest in Christ, you can have no salvation by Christ. He procures salvation for all who are in Him and no other. John 17:12: "Those that thou hast given Me, I have kept, and none of them is lost." If you are without Christ, your condition is like those who were in the old world before the flood: all who were in the ark were saved and preserved, but all who were out of the ark were drowned. Jesus Christ is the ark whereunto every soul that can procure admittance shall be saved; but all who are not in Christ shall be drowned in a river of brimstone which the breath of the Lord shall kindle. You shall be condemned and destroyed forever if you are without Christ. You are without satisfaction from the creature, without acceptance with God, and without salvation by Christ.

And thus, in these six sermons, I have shown you the happiness of a man in Christ, the characters of a man in Christ, and the misery of a man without Christ. And so I have done with this first part of man's misery by nature, and of the first branch of the text, "that at that time you were without Christ."

7

The Second Part of Man's Misery

"Being aliens from the commonwealth of Israel."
Ephesians 2:12

Having finished the first part, I am now to proceed to the second part of man's misery in these words: "Being aliens from the commonwealth of Israel." But before I fall upon this second branch of the text, I shall speak something to you concerning the order of the words, why being without Christ is put in the first place. It is put in the first place to show that as the having of Christ is the foundation and inlet of all happiness and blessedness, so the want of an interest in Christ is the spring and fountain from whence all the miseries and calamities that are incident to the children of men flow. And therefore this, deservedly, is put in the first place, for if you are without Christ, you must be "aliens from the commonwealth of Israel," and "strangers from the covenant of promise, without hope, and without God in the world."

But then, again, why is their being "aliens to the commonwealth of Israel" put in the second place? Because he who is without Christ, the Head, must be without the church, the body, for by the commonwealth of Israel is meant the whole body of the church. They were "aliens from the commonwealth of Israel," that is, the misery of the Ephesians was that they were, while they were in a state of Gentilism, not converted to the faith of Christ by the gospel. They had no interest in the benefits and privileges that the people of God enjoyed who were in the church of Israel. They had none of those spiritual and special privileges and blessings which God bestowed upon all those who were in covenant with Him. They were "aliens to the commonwealth of Israel," that is, they were aliens to the ordinances of God that were then in use in the Jewish church. They were without all the ordinances of Jesus Christ. All the privileges of the people of God the Gentiles wanted before they were in Christ.

Here then you see the complete misery of those who were in a state of Gentilism: they were "aliens to the commonwealth of Israel," and strangers to the divine worship of God which He instituted and appointed in His church, and to all the privileges and prerogatives which the people of God enjoy.

In the words there are two parts observable: first, a description of the church of God, and that by this term, "the commonwealth," the church of God is called "the commonwealth of Israel." Second, here is laid down the alienation of the Ephesians, before conversion, from this church, from this commonwealth.

Now, beloved, from hence I shall only note to you these two observations:

DOCTRINE 1. The church of God is a spiritual commonwealth.

In handling this I shall do these two things: I shall show wherein the church may be compared to a commonwealth, and I shall show you wherein they differ.

The church may be compared to a commonwealth in these four particulars:

1. In a commonwealth there are people of different degrees, ranks, callings, and qualities. All are not princes, nor are all rulers. All are not merchants, nor are all rich. There are men of all degrees, callings, and qualities. Some are rich, some poor; some high, some low; some masters, some servants. Now, in this regard, the church may be compared to a commonwealth, for in the church of God some are high, some low; some rich, some poor; some men grown up to a full stature in Christ, others are but new beginners and babes in Christ; some men are rich in gifts, while others are but poor and mean; some are strong in grace like the oak, while others are but like a broken reed. As it is in a commonwealth, so it is in the church of

God: there are men of several ranks, degrees, callings, qualities, and conditions. 1 Corinthians 12:8–11: All men do not have the same manner of gifts, "for to one is given the word of wisdom, to another the word of knowledge, to another faith, to another the gifts of healing, to another the working of miracles, to another prophecy, to another discerning of spirits, and to another the interpretation of tongues, but all these worketh that one and the selfsame Spirit, dividing to every man severally as He will." As it is in the natural body, so it is in the spiritual body. That body would be a monstrous body if the thumb were as big as the arm, the arm as big as the body, and every part as big as the whole. Just so it is in the church; it is the beauty of it to have a variety of condition.

2. In a commonwealth, though there are multitudes of people, yet they are all governed by one and the same laws, and are all subject to one and the same rulers. So it is in the church of God: though there are many people in it, yet they are all subject to the same laws and are all to walk by the same rule. In this regard it may be compared to a commonwealth, for there is but one rule, the Word of God, that sways the whole church.

3. In a commonwealth it is accounted high treason to subvert or overthrow any law by which that commonwealth is governed; for if it were not so, the laws of a commonwealth would be of no force if any man might break them, add to them, or take from them at his pleasure. And therefore, a commonwealth counts the breaking and violation of their laws to be the greatest injury and dishonor that can be done to them. So it is in the church: the Word of God is very severe in this regard, that if any man shall add or diminish any jot or tittle to or from the Word, God will blot His name out of the book of life.

4. They may be compared one to another in this regard, for as one commonwealth differs from another— they have not both the same rulers, nor the same laws, nor the same customs, nor charters, but differ in everything almost—so the church of God is distinguished from all other parts and people of the world. Commonwealths are

different one from another in four things: in laws, in habits, in languages, and in government. And so is the church of God.

It is different from others in its laws. Law rules in a commonwealth, but only the Word of God rules in the church.

As commonwealths differ from one another in their language, so the Church of God has a language different from all the world. The Church of God speaks the pure language of Canaan, but all the world besides speaks a broken and corrupt language.

As commonwealths differ one from another in regard of habits, so in this regard the Church of God differs from all the world: the Church of God has put on the new man. While all the world has on its old rags still, the Church has put on the long robes of Christ's righteousness, which cover all her nakedness, which all the world is without.

The church of God is different from all others in regard of their government. All kingdoms and commonwealths have men to be their governors, but the Church of God has Christ to be her governor.

Though I have shown you wherein the Church and a commonwealth agree, now I come to show you wherein they differ:

1. They are different in their laws. A commonwealth has laws, acts, and ordinances to govern them, but the church has only the Word of God to be their rule.

2. There is a difference in the extent of those laws. The law of commonwealth only reaches and extends to the outward man. They cannot rule the inward man; therefore we commonly say that our thoughts are free. God only can search the heart and try the reins; but now the law of the Church extends itself to the searching of the soul and spirit, every thought and imagination of the heart. As the apostle says, "The law is spiritual, but I am carnal."

3. There is a difference in regard of the power and efficacy of these laws. The laws of a commonwealth only restrain the outward man if you do amiss, but the law of God

in the Church cannot only restrain in practice, but change the heart, alter the affections, and make you a new man.

4. They differ in this regard: a commonwealth may alter their laws at pleasure if they see occasion. If they find any law grievous or burdensome to the kingdom, they may alter or take it away, and add a new law place of it; but that the Church of God cannot do. The law that the church has now, it must have to the end of the world, God Himself gave the law to His Church, and He cannot give a prejudicial or burdensome law, whereas rulers of commonwealths are but men, and cannot look into the events of things. They are ignorant whether this or that law may be good or not, and therefore change them at their pleasure when they see a necessity. But the rule of the Word of God is an unerring and unalterable rule which all must follow and practice to the end of the world.

5. They differ in their censure. The censure of a commonwealth may extend so far as to confiscation of goods, to banishment, imprisonment, or death, but the censure of the Church extends only to excommunication, or throwing the offender out of their society or fellowship. They can do no more; the Church of Christ can inflict no censure but excommunication; and therefore the practice of those who imprison and censure and inflict punishment upon their people is not warrantable, but contradicts the rule of the Word. Those likewise who cry out against church government as tyrannical greatly err, for the censure of the Church of God is not corporal, but spiritual. But though the Church may not censure any man who is an offender, yet she may complain to the commonwealth, and they may restrain and quell them and keep them under, and inflict punishments upon them.

Thus, then, you see both wherein a church and a commonwealth agree, and wherein they differ. And if it is so that the Church of God is a spiritual commonwealth, then give me leave to draw these three inferences from hence.

Application

USE 1. I may infer from hence the necessity of church government in a church. Did you ever see a commonwealth stand and flourish without rule and laws and order? Order is the staff of a commonwealth. If ever man might do what he lists, and what is right in his own eyes, nothing but ruin and destruction would presently follow. Psalm 11:3: "If the foundations be destroyed, what can the righteous do?" If the laws and foundations of a commonwealth are subverted and destroyed, there will be nothing but ruin. If the Church is a spiritual commonwealth, then there is an absolute necessity of a government in it. And therefore, those who would either rob the church of their government, and would have none at all, or else would introduce a false government upon the church, and do as much as in them lies to overthrow the government of the Church, such as these are to be reproved. Government to a commonwealth is like a hedge to a garden. Suppose you had a very fair garden, and a great many curious flowers and fine slips in it, and one came to you and told you, "Sir, I see many dainty flowers and slips in your garden, but I see none to grow upon your hedge; therefore pull it down; let it grow there no longer." You would say to such a man, "No, by no means; for though nothing grows upon the hedge, yet the hedge preserves the flowers that grow in the garden, and keeps them from the violences of wild beasts." So though a government in the church does not make us holy (a man may go to heaven without a government), yet is it exceedingly necessary to preserve the Church of God.

USE 2. I may infer from the Church's being a spiritual commonwealth the necessity of union in the Church. Commonwealths are preserved by union. You see what four year's war have brought upon our kingdom: it has almost destroyed the face of our commonwealth. Union are the sinews and ligaments of a commonwealth. If men are disunited and disjointed, that commonwealth cannot subsist. "A kingdom divided against itself cannot stand." The Church of God being a spiritual commonwealth argues the great necessity of unity in the Church and the great danger of division. The Church of God cannot be safe without union. I must tell you (to the grief of our hearts it is spoken) that there was never less unity in the Church of God, since the very first plantation of it by the apostles in the primitive times, than there is at this day, wherein every man almost is set one against another.

Truly I look upon it as a very sad omen and prediction that God is bringing upon us the most dismal persecution that ever yet our eyes beheld. I have read in *The Book of Martyrs* that the coming in of the eighth persecution was occasioned by the division and falling out of Christians one with another. I wish it may not be so with us, beloved. It is ordinary among a great many men to cry out and exclaim against the ministers of the gospel, as if they were the great incendiaries and causers of divisions and dissensions amongst you; but I would have you know that those who preach against division are not dividers, but those who make divisions are dividers. The apostle said, "Mark them that cause divisions among you, and avoid them." Those men who have caused divisions, and brought in strange opinions, sects, and schisms into the land are the make-bates of the nation. The staff of union and the staff of beauty—when one is broken, the other is broken.

I have read a story of a man who had fourscore children, and lying upon his deathbed he caused his children to come before him, and desired that a bundle of small rods might be brought to him. His children began to wonder among themselves what his design and purpose in doing it was; but when they had brought them, their father commanded every one of his sons, beginning from the youngest to the eldest, to take the bundle and try which of them could break it, but none of them was found able to do it. At last, taking the bundle himself, he unbound it, breaking the sticks one by one, till he had broken them all. "And now, my children," he said, "this I do to teach you that if you combine and keep close together in unity like a bundle of sticks, none will be able to break you or do you any harm; but if you divide and fall off one from another, you will soon be ruined and broken in pieces." So if the members of the Church of God would unite and partake of public ordinances together, hear, pray, and perform holy duties together, and still remain conjoined in one, we need not fear the power or policy of any to do us any harm.

USE 3. If the church is a spiritual commonwealth, then I may infer further the necessity of our laboring to improve the Church's interest in a commonwealth. Nature will teach men to labor to preserve and advance the good and benefit of the commonwealth. Every man will contribute for the good of the body politic, and therefore let us labor to promote the Church's interest.

DOCTRINE 2. It is a great misery for a man to be a stranger to the true Church of God. You may be in the true Church, and yet not of the true Church. As ill humors in a man's body are in the body, though not in the constituent parts of the body, so you may be in the Church, and of the Church visible too, and yet not be of the members of the Church invisible, of the Church of the first born. You may not partake of the special spiritual privileges of the church of God.

1. Wicked men are strangers to the effectual calling of the church. 1 Peter 2:21: "Ye are called with a holy calling," which wicked men are without.

2. They are strangers to the comforts of the Church of God; they lack those joys and comforts that the people of God enjoy.

3. They are strangers to a Christian communion in the Church. A wicked man does not know how to manage a spiritual communion with the people of God.

USE. Now if it is so that wicked men are strangers to the Church of God in the spiritual benefits and privileges they have by Christ, then by way of use I shall only draw from hence these two inferences.

Do not lay too much dependence and confidence

upon being members of the Church. You may be under the outward and common mercies, and yet want the inward and spiritual benefits of the Church of God. There is many a man who is born and brought up in the Church of England, and yet, notwithstanding, is unable to give any ground of his salvation by Christ. You may have the Church of England to be your mother and yet never have God to be your Father. I do not speak this to the disparagement of the Church of England, for Christ and salvation by Him is to be had in England as well as elsewhere. I would not have you think that England is no true Church, for it is a Church of Jesus Christ; but I do say that you may be of this church, and born and bred in this church, and partake of all the ordinances and outward privileges in this church, and yet never come to heaven. For, as the apostle said, "All are not Israel that are of Israel."

If it is so, then this may be a matter of reprehension to wicked men, who see they are in the church yet they are not of the Church of Jesus Christ. You are in the church, but as a wen, a botch, or blain is in the body, you are a blemish to the church of God. Wicked men are spots and blemishes in the church, as in 2 Peter 2:13. Though they are in the church, yet they are a burden to the church; and I wish that godly men counted it a greater burden to them than they do, that there are so many wicked men in their church. A wicked man in the church is like a wooden leg to the body of a man, a natural leg that carries the body; but if a man has a wooden leg, the body must carry it. So wicked men are a great burden and trouble to the church. As Paul said (speaking of wicked men), "I wish they were even cut off that trouble you." Such men as are loose in practice and loose in opinion, truly both these have been great burdens and troublers to the Church of God. They are to the Church as Jonah was to the ship: what a storm have they raised in this kingdom! God knows whether you or I shall ever live to see it blow over. Thus much for the second part of man's misery by nature: "That at that time ye were aliens to the commonwealth of Israel."

8

Strangers from the Covenants of Promise

"And strangers from the covenants of promise."
Ephesians 2:12

We come now to the third part: "And strangers from the covenants of promise." But before I draw out any doctrines from these words, I shall resolve these five questions which are very needful to be discussed.

QUESTION 1. What is the difference between the covenants and the promise? For many look upon them to be both one and the same thing.

ANSWER. In answer to this, you must know that, though every covenant is a promise, yet every promise is not a covenant. A covenant is a more comprehensive thing than a promise, for a covenant is nothing but a bundle of promises. All the promises in the gospel are bound up together in a bundle, so that herein you see the difference between a covenant and a promise.

QUESTION. 2. What is meant by the covenants of promise?

ANSWER. It is the free and gracious promise that God made with Adam after the fall, and with the patriarchs, Abraham, Isaac, and Jacob, and all the faithful, wherein He promised them salvation and eternal life through Christ who was to come. This is the covenant of promise, even the promise which God made with His children before the coming of Christ, wherein He covenanted to give them life and salvation through Christ who was promised to come.

QUESTION 3. Why is it called the covenants of promise?

ANSWER. It is so called because Christ, the matter of

70

this covenant, had not actually come, but only promised that He would come; that is the reason of this phrase here, the covenants of promise.

QUESTION. 4. Why is it called in the plural number, the covenants of promise, seeing there was but one covenant of grace? The covenant of works was made with Adam before the fall, and the covenant of grace after the fall.

ANSWER. It is called the covenants of promise, not as if there were several kinds of covenants and salvation by Christ, but because there were various exhibitions and administrations of this one covenant; not as if this covenant were many in kind and substance, for it is the same now that it was at the beginning, but only that it was diversely administered, explained, and enlarged. Sometimes it is called a new covenant, that is, new in regard of the urging and exhibition of it. The like phrase you have touching love: "Behold, a new command I give unto you, that you love one another." It was called new because it was then newly enforced upon the people. The tenor of the covenant of grace is that we shall have life and salvation through the blood of Christ. It is called covenants because it was so often renewed and administered. First it was made with Adam after his fall: "The seed of the woman shall bruise the serpent's head," and then it was renewed to Abraham, as Paul explained in Hebrews 3, and after him to Isaac, and then to Jacob, David, Solomon, and all the faithful. But the covenant, for substance, was still the same, though it was many times renewed; and so it continues the same to this very day. Thus you have a brief account of these four queries.

QUESTION 5. What is it to be a stranger to the covenants of promise?

ANSWER. Did you but dive and look into the bottom of it, you would find it to be the final upshot of the misery of an unconverted man. To be "a stranger to the covenants of promise" is to be in such a dismal and lamentable and deplorable condition that none of all the promises of God for grace and life and salvation by Christ pertains to him. And is not this a very miserable and sad condition, that the Lord looks upon a man in an unregenerate state as incapable of any mercy, life, or salvation by Christ? A covenant, as I told you, is a bundle of promises; it contains all the promises of grace, life, and salvation. Now if you are without the covenant, you must be destitute of all the promises by Christ.

Thus, having by way of premise opened these five particulars, I shall now draw out this one observation from the words.

DOCTRINE. All men, during the time of their unregeneracy, are strangers to the covenants of grace, so that they can lay no just claim to any promise of having life and salvation by Christ.

You are strangers to the covenants of promise; and, beloved, when I tell you that you have no title to any one promise of life or salvation by Christ, it is the saddest news that ever you can open your ears to hear. If you are a stranger to the covenant, you are without all the promises, for the covenant is a bundle of promises, all the promises of God bound up together. In handling this point, I shall only show you two things and then apply them. I shall show you what the covenant of grace is. I shall show you how you may know whether you are men without the covenant of grace or not, and can lay no just claim to any promise of life and salvation by Christ. And I shall wind up all in a practical use, both for consolation to those who are in the covenant, and for terror to those who have no right to the covenant.

1. The covenant of grace is that free and gracious covenant which God made with Adam after the fall, promising him pardon of sin and eternal life, through the righteousness of Jesus Christ. This is the sum and substance of the covenant of grace: it is the promise of God first made to Adam, and then renewed to Abraham, Isaac, Jacob, David, Solomon, and all the faithful. It is the solemn promise that God made to the elect of their obtaining salvation through the righteousness of Jesus Christ: Now here you must be very careful lest you run into a mis-

take, for there are two sorts of people who run into very dangerous errors concerning this particular.

The Socinians are of the opinion that none of the patriarchs and good men in the Old Testament went to heaven till Christ came in the flesh, which is a very uncharitable and ungodly opinion.

There are others who hold that living in obedience to the moral law of Moses tied the people to the covenant of works to be justified by it. They hold that the Jews did not live under a covenant of grace till Christ came, but, if it were so, none of them could possibly be saved, for "by the works of the law shall no flesh living be justified." No man in the world can ever go to heaven by the covenant of works. This I do only mention, by the way, that you may see and understand that, since the fall of Adam, all men are saved by the covenant of grace. The covenant of works was no longer in force while Adam lived and continued in innocence, but as soon as ever he fell, the gospel was presently preached unto them as well as it is to us now. It was preached unto them more darkly, however, and to us more clearly. Christ was preached unto them as the One to come, but He is preached unto us as having come already.

2. We come now to stir you up and put you upon inquiry as to how you may know whether you are the people who are in covenant with God or not, so that you can lay a just claim to the covenant of grace and all the promises therein contained for salvation and life eternal by Christ. I shall handle this query not in the positive, but in the negative part of it, how you may know that you are not in the covenant of grace. I shall give you three or four discoveries of it.

First, you, O man, are not in covenant with God if you have not yet broken the league and covenant you made with your lusts. You who still keep up and maintain the league and covenant with your lusts and corruptions have not as yet come within the covenant of grace. That man who makes a covenant with death and hell cannot be under the covenant of grace, and therefore you who have

not broken off with your sins by repentance and righteousness, and with your iniquities by showing mercy, you
who are in a wicked course and resolve to continue so, lay
no claim to the covenant of grace. You who are engaged
to your lusts, you who have been bad and will be so still,
you have no interest in the covenant of grace.

Second, you who think to be saved by a covenant of
works cannot be under a covenant of grace. You who hope
to be justified by works are fallen from grace, as the apostle says in Galatians 5:4; that is, not that you are fallen
from the habit of grace, you are fallen from the doctrine
of grace, which holds out justification by Christ. That man
shall never be saved by Christ who thinks he cannot be
saved by Christ; and therefore a papist, living and dying in
this very opinion, that he must be saved by a covenant of
works, cannot be saved. If you are not cast out of yourselves so as to rely wholly and only upon Christ for life and
salvation, you can lay no just claim to being under the
covenant of grace.

Third, you are strangers to the covenant of grace who
make no conscience of breaking the engagements and
promises you have made to God. You who are careless of
keeping the covenants you have made with God, this is an
evident demonstration that you are not in covenant with
God. Those who are in covenant with God make conscience of keeping their covenants with God. If in times of
affliction and trouble you make large promises to God of
better obedience, and yet afterwards return with the dog
to his vomit, and are bad or worse than ever you were, this
argues that you have no interest at all in the covenant of
grace.

Application

Thus I have done with the second query, the discoveries of those who are not in the covenant of grace. I have
only now the application of the point to speak to, and the
use that I shall make of it shall be, first, for consolation to

all who are in the covenant of grace. You have a bundle of promises to which you may have recourse, and lay claim to them as your own. I shall make use of it, second, by way of terror, to show the misery of those who are strangers to this covenant of grace.

This may be a matter of great consolation to you who are under the covenant of grace, who are in covenant with God. This should provoke you to joy and comfort in the consideration of the great happiness you enjoy in being under the covenant of grace, compared to the misery you would be exposed to if you lived under a covenant of works. And now, beloved, lend me your thoughts a little, while I show you in fourteen particulars the great happiness you are now in, being in covenant with God under a covenant of grace, compared to the misery you would have lain under in being only under a covenant of works. Do this and live. I shall but name them to you, and run over them very briefly.

1. The covenant of works was given by God as a Creator to Adam, but the covenant of grace is given by God as a Father to a believer. God did not have this term of a Father before the fall, only of a God and Creator; but, being under a covenant of grace, you may look upon that God, who was only a creator to Adam, as a Father to you.

2. This would have been your misery under a covenant of works, for it exacts perfect obedience, and punishes the offender in case of disobedience; but being under a covenant of grace, the Lord accepts, through Christ, sincere obedience, though it is not perfect.

3. The covenant of works is not content with perfect obedience, unless it is personal. It must not only be perfect, but it must be done by you in your own person. But the covenant of grace accepts perfect obedience, even though it is not done by you, but in the person of Jesus Christ. God the Father as fully accepts Christ obeying and fulfilling His will in doing and suffering in our behalf as if we had done and suffered what He did in our own persons; and herein lies the great happiness of a man under the covenant of grace.

4. The covenant of works was made by God to Adam without a mediator. There was no third person between God and Adam; but the covenant of grace was made by God with us in the hand of a mediator, Jesus Christ. You may conceive it thus: suppose two men were at discord and variance one with another, and a third person, a friend to both these who were fallen out, came and endeavored to decide the difference, first going to one, and desiring him to be reconciled to the other, and then going to the second, and entreating him to be pacified towards the first, till he had united and reconciled them both together.

So it is here. Christ is a friend both to God and man. He is the Son of God and He is husband of His Church. And being the Mediator of the new covenant, He comes first to His Father and says, "Father, I know that all mankind has broken that first covenant which they made with Thee, and are thereby justly liable to all that wrath and punishment due to the breach of it. I know Thy anger and displeasure against them, but I pray, O Father, be reconciled and well pleased with Thy people; give them the sanctification of their natures while they live here, and give them heaven and happiness when they die."

Then Christ comes to believers and tells them, "Sirs, I have procured peace, pardon, and reconciliation for you, the sanctification of your natures here, and heaven when you die. Therefore, lift up your heads with joy." Christ first goes to His Father and sues Him for pardon, and then comes to us and begs us to be comforted.

5. Adam, under the covenant of works, had nothing but works to save him. He was to keep this covenant of works only by his own strength; he had no strength but his own to perform any duty; he had no bottom or foundation but himself to stand on. But under the covenant of grace we are kept by "the mighty power of God through faith unto salvation." We are under a far better condition under the covenant of grace than Adam was in the state of innocence, for, though he was perfectly holy, yet he was not immutably holy. But now the foundation of God

stands sure: we are kept by the mighty power of God unto salvation.

6. The covenant of works, if a man once broke it, admitted no repentance. Had Adam and Eve, after the fall, wept their eyes out or prayed their hearts out, all would have done them no good. Repentance will no way avail the covenant of works. This is just as it is in the civil law: if a man has committed murder, the law does not inquire whether the man has repented, or is sorry for what he has done or not; the law takes notice whether he has done the act or not. If he has, he must die; no repentance will avail. But in the covenant of grace, it is far otherwise, for though you have done the act and broken God's commandments, yet if you repent and mourn and grieve for the sins you have committed against God, the Lord will pardon and forgive them as if they had never been committed. So this is another great happiness you enjoy in being under the covenant of grace.

7. Since Adam was under the covenant of works, God took the very first forfeiture or breaking of this covenant, and one sin made God to disannul that covenant; whereas the covenant of grace is not made void nor disannulled though you commit many sins. In Romans 5:16–17 the apostle says, "Not as it was by one that sinned so is the gift, for the judgment was by one to condemnation, but the free gift is of many offenses unto justification." That is, under the covenant of works, one sin condemned all the world; but under the covenant of grace, the free gift is of many offenses unto justification. Many sins are pardoned and many offenses are passed over. The covenant of grace pardons many sins and overlooks many weaknesses and failings. Though you break your covenant often, time after time, yet the covenant of grace shall not be broken. The first covenant was disannulled for one sin, but the second covenant shall not be disannulled for many sins, as you may see in Psalm 89:31–34, where God says, "If they break My statues, and keep not My commandments, then I will visit their transgressions with the rod, and their iniquity with stripes. Nevertheless My loving-kindness will I not ut-

terly take from him, nor suffer My faithfulness to fail. My covenant will I not break, nor alter the thing that is gone out of My lips." Psalm 111:5: "Will the Lord ever be mindful of His covenant." So this is another part of your happiness.

8. Pray observe, had Adam continued still under the covenant of works, and kept the covenant, performing exact and perfect obedience to it, yet he could never have come to heaven. He would have had an everlasting continuance in paradise, but he would never have enjoyed heaven. But being under the covenant of grace entitles you to everlasting salvation and happiness in heaven by Jesus Christ.

9. Under the covenant of works, though God promised life to Adam upon the performing of the covenant, yet He did not promise pardon to Adam upon the breach of the covenant. God promised him this: "Do this and you shall live"; but God did not promise him that though he should break His commands and sin against Him, yet he would be saved notwithstanding. In the covenant of works, there is no promise at all of pardon, only of life; but under the covenant of grace you have a double promise: You shall obtain life eternal and salvation by Christ, and you shall have all your sins pardoned and washed away in the blood of Christ that you commit against him. You shall have pardon and remission of sins by Christ, so that no sin shall be charged upon you.

10. Under the covenant of works, God accepted the person for the work's sake; but under the covenant of grace He accepts the work for the person's sake. And herein lies our happiness: under the covenant of works, God accepted Adam's person merely because his works were altogether righteous and good. He accepted his person no farther than his works were good, for as soon as he broke the command, God was displeased with him. But under the covenant of grace, God accepts the works for the person's sake. Abel was first accepted and then the sacrifice; first his person was well pleasing to God, and then the sacrifice for the person's sake. So God accepts

our praying, reading, hearing, and all that we do through Jesus Christ. Being well pleased with our persons in Christ, He is delighted and well pleased with all our services in Him.

11. The covenant of works was made to all men generally and universally without exception, but the covenant of grace was made only to a select and chosen people. All mankind was in Adam under a covenant of works. If Adam had kept the law, all mankind would have lived by him; but herein lies your happiness in being under the covenant of grace when it is made only to a few, to a peculiar and chosen number of men.

12. The covenant of works entitles men to no further honor than to be a worthy and honorable servant of God, not a child of God; but under the covenant of grace, we not only become servants, but adopted sons. We are the children of promise by faith in Christ; the covenant of grace puts us into a state of sonship. Adam was the son of God by creation, but not by grace and adoption till the covenant of grace was made.

13. Creation was the foundation of the covenant of works, but it is redemption that is the foundation of the covenant of grace. The foundation is that Christ has died and shed His blood for us.

14. In the covenant of works, God only manifested the attributes of His greatness, power, wisdom, and justice; but in the covenant of grace He demonstrates the attributes of His grace and mercy, goodness and patience. God, in the covenant of works, was only a just God. "Do this and live. As long as you keep My commandments you shall live and no longer." But in the covenant of grace, He is a merciful God too. The Lord made the attributes of His mercy and goodness to shine forth in this covenant. Should God say to us, "As long as you do well, it will be well with you, but if ever you break one command or commit one sin, you shall be damned," we would be in a most miserable and undone condition, and could not escape damnation. But since we are under the covenant of grace, by His Son Jesus Christ He tells us that, although we break His com-

mands and sin against Him, yet in His Son He will pardon us and pass by all our transgressions as if they had never been committed.

9

Dread and Terror to Those Who Are Strangers from the Covenant of Promise

"And strangers from the covenants of promise."
Ephesians 2:12

I have shown you in fourteen particulars your great happiness in being under the covenant of grace compared to the misery you would have lain under had you been under the covenant of works. I come now to the second use, which is a use of dread and terror, to lay before you the great misery of those who are strangers to this covenant of promise. And here I might lay before you much astonishing and perplexing matter to all those who are not in the covenant of grace. I shall be the larger upon this particular, because the last day I spent half an hour about a use of comfort, in showing you your happiness in being under the covenant of grace. Therefore, now, I shall spend the like time in declaring the misery of all those who are strangers to the covenant, which I shall comprise under six heads.

1. This is one part of your misery: you are bound to keep the whole law of God, and that in your own persons, else you can never be saved. Oh, how impossible is this for any to do! He who is under the covenant of grace, God the Father accepts Christ's keeping and fulfilling of the law for him as if it were done by him in his own person. But to such as are not in this covenant of grace God says, "If you do not keep the whole law, and that personally, you shall be damned eternally." In Galatians 5:3, the apostle says, "I testify again to every man that is circumcised, that he is a debtor to do the whole law." If you will not accept Christ and salvation by His blood alone, but run to

circumcision, I tell you, said the apostle, that "you are
debtors to keep the whole law of God," and He will cast
you into hell upon the least breach of the law. Oh, you
unhappy man, upon how hard terms can you hope for salvation, even upon impossible terms! You can as well keep
the sea in your fist as keep the whole law of God in your
own person. God says to you, "If you break but one command, though you should keep all the rest, yet you shall
die and be damned eternally; but if you are under the
covenant of grace, though you break the law again and
again, yet Christ redeems you from the curse of the law,
being made a curse for you."

2. You who are a stranger to the covenant of grace, you
have no strength but your own to help you in the dis-
charge of all your duties; but a man who is under the
covenant of grace, God commands him a duty, and with
the command gives him power to perform the duty. God
bids him act grace, and pours upon him a spirit of grace;
he bids him pray, and gives him a spirit of prayer. God
commands him a duty, and gives him a flexible, willing,
obedient heart, and abilities to perform the duty. When in
Scripture God commands a duty, He likewise promises to
assist and enable us to the performance of the duty. For
example, the Lord bids us to wash ourselves and make
ourselves clean, and put away the evil of our doings. A
poor soul says, "Oh, Lord, I am not able to wash my heart,
nor cleanse my ways, nor do anything that is good of myself." And therefore, says God again, "I will wash you and
make you whiter than snow." So God bids us to get new
hearts, and then again He promises to create in us new
hearts, and renew right spirits within us.

But this is your unhappiness, O man who is a stranger
to the covenant of grace: God bids you keep His commands, but He gives you no power to fulfill His commands. He bids you act grace, and never gives you a spirit
of grace. He bids you pray, and yet never pours out upon
you a spirit of prayer. And if Adam in his innocence was
not able to keep God's commands, how much more unable are you to do anything that may please God? You, by

your own strength, are as able to make a world as to make one prayer or perform any duty in a holy and spiritual manner. You can as well destroy the whole world with your own hands as subdue any lust by your own strength. But under the covenant of grace, God tells us that, though we cannot keep the law, yet He will accept His Son's keeping it for us. And He has promised to help and assist us in the performance of everything that He commands.

3. You who are strangers to the covenant of grace, herein lies your misery: you have no advocate to plead for you, nor mediator to stand between God and you. You have an angry God frowning upon you, a galled conscience ready to accuse you, and everything else in the world against you, but no friend, either in heaven or in earth, to plead or speak for you. Christ is a Mediator to those only who are under a covenant of grace. Now what can you say for yourself, O man? Why should you not be condemned and damned in hell forever for your drunkenness, adultery, Sabbath-breaking, profaneness, swearing, lying, and ungodly practices? You can have nothing to plead for yourself, but you must be cast out into hellfire irrecoverably.

But a godly man who is under the covenant of grace can say, "Lord, here is Christ, my Mediator, who is pleading with Thee for the pardon of all my sins, and for the obtaining of heaven, happiness, and glory for me through His obedience and merits." But you who are under the covenant of works cannot say, "I have Christ to plead for me, and to be an Advocate with the Father, to beg for pardon of sin, and life and salvation for me." You cannot say so, for without the covenant of grace there is no mediator. Christ is the Mediator only of the new covenant. Therefore, what a sad condition are you in, seeing as verily as you stand there now, you must one day stand before God's tribunal to answer and be judged for everything you have done in your body, whether it is good or evil. Then you will have nobody to plead for you, but must inevitably be cast into everlasting burnings.

4. Being out of the covenant of grace, this is your mis-

ery: God will, in exactness and rigor of justice, proceed
against you for your sins without any mixture of mercy at
all. Beloved, God has no mercy without His covenant, but
in the covenant of grace He is "a God gracious and merciful, slow to anger, and of great kindness, abundant in
mercy and truth, pardoning iniquity, transgressions and
sins." But He is clothed with justice and rigor to all who
are outside this covenant. As it is in courts of judicature in
point of life and death, the judge will take no notice
whether the man is a sorrowful man or not. The law is not
to show mercy, but to punish the offense; the law does not
inquire whether the man is penitent and sorry for what he
has done, but whether the act is done or not. If it is, he
must die for it; there is no remedy. Just so it is here: God
does not inquire, under a covenant of works, whether you
are sorrowful for breaking His law, but He inquires
whether you have broken it or not. If you have, He will
condemn you and cast you into hellfire. Then the poor
soul cries out, "Oh, Lord, be merciful to me this once. It
shall be a warning to me. I will never sin against Thee, nor
displease Thee more, but will from henceforth walk more
humbly, holily, and circumspectly before Thee." And yet,
all this that you have promised, if you were able to perform it, will not avail you, for God will hear none out of
Christ, and out of the covenant of grace.

5. A man out of the covenant of grace has no true and
special title to any of the blessings of God here in this
world. God's blessings go along with His covenant, and
therefore it is very observable that in that chapter where
God promises the blessings of the covenant of grace, in
that very chapter He promises the blessings of this life, as
you may see in Ezekiel 36. God says there: "I will sprinkle
clean water upon you, and ye shall be clean, yea, from all
your filthiness, and from all your idols will I cleanse you; a
new heart will I also give you, and a new spirit will I put
within you, and will take away the stony heart from out of
your flesh. And I will give you a heart of flesh, and will put
my Spirit within you, and cause you to walk in My statutes,
and ye shall keep My judgments and do them, and you

shall dwell in the land that I gave to your fathers, and ye shall be My people, and I will be your God." All these are the mercies of the covenant of grace. Now mark the next words: "I will call for corn, and will increase it, and lay no famine upon you, and I will multiply the fruit of the tree, and the increase of the field." And so the 10th and 11th verses of that chapter read: "And I will multiply men upon you. . .and the cities shall be inhabited, and the wastes shall be builded, and I will multiply upon man and beast, and they shall increase and bring fruit, and I will do better unto you than at your beginnings, and ye shall know that I am the Lord." Here the Lord entails earthly blessings to the covenant of grace, intimating that all who are under the covenant of grace have a title not only to all spiritual blessings, but to temporal blessings likewise. But no wicked man out of the covenant of grace has any true title to any outward blessings. Those who are of the faithful are blessed with faithful Abraham, and enjoy outward blessings as a blessing; but wicked men, it is true, have something allowed them, but it is as to prisoners. In a prison they have something to keep them alive until their execution; and so wicked men have prison allowances till their execution day.

6. The misery of those who are strangers to the covenant of grace lies in this: God will not give acceptance to any of your services, though you may do as much, for the matter of them, as any godly man does. Nay, you may hear more sermons, say more prayers, and perform more duties than a godly man does, and yet not be accepted, while the others shall, as you may see in Genesis 4:4–5. Cain and Abel both brought sacrifices to God, one of his flock and the other of his grounds. And the apostle, speaking of this, says that "by faith Abel offered a more excellent sacrifice than Cain." It was not more excellent in regard of it, for in all probability and likelihood Cain's sacrifice was of more value than Abel's, since his was but a few young lambs, the firstlings of his flock. Cain's was of the first fruits of the ground, and yet Abel's sacrifice was accepted and the other's rejected, because Abel was a godly man

under the covenant of grace, by which God accepted what
he did, though it was less than Cain's. Solomon said, "The
sacrifice of the wicked is an abomination to the Lord, but
the prayer of the upright is His delight." A sacrifice, you
know, is a great deal more costly than a prayer, for that
costs a man nothing but his breath, while the other will
cost a great deal of money; and yet a costly sacrifice is
hated by God, coming from a wicked man, while a penniless prayer coming from a godly man is accepted. So under the covenant of grace, though you do less for the matter of the duty than wicked men do, yet yours shall be accepted while theirs shall be rejected.

Thus I have done with the use of terror in laying down
to you this six-fold misery of those men who are strangers
to the covenant of grace. And here, because I would not
have any poor soul who is under the covenant of grace,
and partaker of all the great privileges of it, to go away
with a sad heart, I shall only leave with you two or three
words of comfort. You children of the covenant, who are
under the covenant of grace, let not your hearts be troubled at what has been said this day concerning the misery
of those men who are strangers to this covenant. And to
bear up and support your spirits, I shall give you two or
three comfortable considerations.

1. All outward blessings that you enjoy come to you in
a covenant way. God has given you these blessings as an
appendix to the covenant, and by virtue of an entail to His
covenant. The Lord never gives you a common blessing,
but you see the love of a Father, a husband, and a friend,
and the love of God in that blessing. Therefore, as I told
you before, in that very chapter where God promises the
blessings of the covenant of grace, He promises the blessings of this life, too, as an entail to the covenant. Wicked
men may have blessings, but not by virtue of a promise,
not by virtue of the covenant of grace.

But now, if you ask me how you may know whether the
blessings you enjoy come to you by virtue of the covenant
of grace, I answer, you may know it by these two things:

You may know whether the blessings you enjoy come to you by virtue of the covenant of grace if you use and employ all the blessing you receive from God to the honor of God. Thus Abraham did, as you may see in Genesis 17:1, 2, 8, 12. His using the blessings of God to promote the service of God demonstrated that those blessings came to him from God in a covenant way; but those who are strangers to this covenant, the mercies they enjoy are given them for their hurt.

When blessings are as cords to draw you nearer to God, and as bands to tie you fast to God, then they come to you in a covenant way. Jeremiah 31:11–12: "For the Lord hath redeemed Jacob, and ransomed him from the hand of him that is stronger than he. Therefore they shall come and sing in the height of Zion, and shall flow together to the goodness of the Lord, for the wheat, and for the wine, and for the oil, and for the young of the flock and of the herd." That is, all the mercies of God shall make them to come nearer and nearer, and cleave closer to God. You then who enjoy your share of the blessings of God, if they do not endear you and draw you nearer to God, you cannot look upon them as flowing in upon you in a covenant way.

2. You who are in covenant with God, know this for your comfort: the Lord accepts the little that you do in His service better than a great deal that a wicked man performs to Him. God will accept a few turtle doves from you, while He will not accept one thousand rams, or ten hundred thousand rivers of oil from the wicked. He will accept a cup of cold water given to a righteous man in the name of a righteous man, when He will not accept the costliest sacrifice from the wicked. Oh, what a happy condition are you in who are under the covenant of grace! Wicked men may hear more sermons, perform more duties, and say more prayers to God than you, and yet in all their duties be rejected while you are accepted.

3. Take this for your comfort: whenever you offend God, and provoke Him to anger, you have a Mediator to stand between God and you. Though you are guilty, yet

you have an Advocate to plead your cause for you. You
who are under the covenant of grace may say to Christ
your Mediator, as the Israelites said to Moses when they
had offended God: "Go thou and speak unto God for us."
So may you say. When you have nothing but thundering
and lightning and tempests in your souls, and the flashing
of hellfire in your consciences, then you may say to Christ,
"Go now to God and speak for me; mediate with Thy Father for the pardon of all my sins. I have offended God,
oh, intercede with Him on my behalf. I have committed a
great offense, oh, plead with Thy Father and beg a pardon
for me." This you may say to Christ, being under the
covenant of grace.

But here, lest anyone should lie under a spiritual delusion, and think himself under the covenant of grace when
he is a stranger to it, lest the dogs should snatch at the
children's meat, I shall lay down to you some distinguishing characters whereby you may know whether you are
under the covenant of grace or not. And before I make
entrance upon this, I will only premise four sad and dismal conclusions that will make way the better for what I
have to handle in the examination.

Take this conclusion: a man may be within the outward and common privileges of the covenant of grace,
and yet be without the saving and spiritual privileges of it,
such as pardon of sin, having God to be your God, and
Christ to be your Savior. In Deuteronomy 29:10–12, Moses
says, "Ye stand this day all of you before the Lord your
God, your captains of your tribes, your elders, and your
officers, with all the men of Israel, your little ones, your
wives, and thy stranger that is in thy camp, from the hewer
of thy wood, unto the drawer of thy water, that thou
shouldst enter into covenant with the Lord thy God." Now
here you see, all, from the rich to the poor, were to enter
into covenant with God, and yet it is not imaginable that
all these partook of the inward privileges of the covenant
of grace. They all partook of circumcision, which was the
seal of the covenant, of the outward privileges of it, but
not all did partake of the inward and special mercies of

the covenant of grace, such as pardon of sin, peace of conscience, joy in believing God to be their God, and Christ to be their Savior. So in Romans 9:4–5, the apostle says, "They are Israelites to whom pertaineth the adoption, and the glory, and the covenants, and the giving of the law, and the service of God, and the promises, of whose are the fathers, and of whom as concerning the flesh Christ came." These were very great privileges, and yet verse 8: "These are not all the children of God." Though they had the external blessings of the covenant, yet they were not all the children of God. So you see that you may be within the Church of God, and partake of the outward blessings of the covenant, and yet want the inward and spiritual blessings of it.

Take this sad conclusion: most men in the world are without the common and outward mercies of the covenant of grace, as are all who are in the state of Judaism, Turkism, and paganism; and these being without the outward privileges of the Church, they can hope for no salvation. If you should divide the world into one and thirty parts, there is but a fifth part of them who are Christians. There are nineteen parts of the world that are Jews and Turks, and seven parts that are pagans. So there are but five parts that are Christians. Most men in the world are without the outward and common blessings of the covenant of grace, and therefore can obtain no salvation by Christ.

Take this conclusion yet further: most of those men who are within the outward and common blessings are yet without the saving and spiritual blessings and privileges of the covenant of grace. This conclusion is answerable to that phrase in Matthew 22:14: "Many are called, but few are chosen." There are but a few chosen to life and happiness among those who are partakers of the external mercies of the covenant of grace. Zechariah 13:8–9: "And it shall come to pass, that in all the land, saith the Lord, two parts therein shall be shut off and die, but the third shall be left therein, and I will bring the third part through the fire, and will refine them as silver is refined,

and will try them as gold is tried; they shall call on my
name and I will hear them; I will say, it is my people, and
they shall say, the Lord is my God." There was but one
part of three that were godly, and as it was then, so it is
now: there is but one part of three that can say truly they
have an interest in the covenant of grace, and therefore,
beloved, this may be some of your lot. There are many of
you who have a share in the outward blessings of the
covenant, who have the ordinances and means of grace
and make profession of Christ, and yet few of you who
have any special and peculiar blessing from Christ. When
Christ was thronged in the multitude, there were a great
many who touched Him, but one only who got any virtue
from Him. Just so there are a very few who enjoy the special and peculiar blessings of the covenant—to have sin
pardoned, their corruptions subdued, their duties and
services accepted, God to be their God, and Christ to be
their Savior.

Take this conclusion likewise: such is the pride and
deceitfulness of man's heart naturally, that from their being within the compass of the outward blessings of the
covenant they will conclude themselves to have an interest
in the inward and spiritual blessings of the covenant of
grace. This you shall find the Jews did in John 8:33, 39, 41.
In verse 33 they say that they are the seed of Abraham.
Verse 39: "Abraham is our father." And from hence they
conclude in verse 41 that God was their father too, though
Christ told them plainly they were of their father the devil.
Wicked men are very apt to deceive themselves and think
they have an interest in the spiritual blessing of the covenant of grace because they partake of the sacraments and
outward ordinances; whereas in baptism you may have
your face sprinkled with water, and yet never have your
hearts sprinkled with the blood of Christ. You may be
born in the church, and yet never be of the church of the
first-born in heaven; you may have the church to be your
mother, and yet never have God to be your Father. There
is but a remnant according to the election of grace; the
main body is cast away. There is but a remnant saved, and

yet the Jews boasted that because they had the adoption, the glory, the covenant, and the promise, therefore God was theirs too, and heaven and happiness and all theirs, when there was no such matter.

10

How to Know If You Belong to the Covenant of Grace

"And strangers from the covenants of promise."
Ephesians 2:12

I formerly premised four conclusions so that you might not harbor any secret conjectures and imaginations that you belong to the covenant of grace when you do not. I come now to give you some trials and discoveries whereby you may know whether you can lay a just claim to life and salvation from God through His son Jesus Christ, by virtue of His promise. You may know whether you belong to the covenant of grace or not under these three headings:

If you partake of the spiritual blessings of the covenant.

If you have the inseparable consequences of the covenant.

If you perform the conditions of the covenant of grace, which is faith: believe and be saved.

If you have these three, you may lay an undoubted claim to the covenant of grace.

The first discovery of being in the covenant of grace is if you have the saving and spiritual blessings of the covenant of grace, which are these four:

1. God will be your God and you shall be His people. This is the tenor of the covenant of grace. Jeremiah 31:33: "I will be their God, and they shall be My people." I shall open this blessing to you a little, for God to be our God. It notes these three things:

First, for God to be your God notes that God is yours

in a special way of propriety, which none but those who are the children of God can have. Wicked men cannot lay claim to God as their God. When Pharaoh desired Moses to pray for him, said he, "I have sinned against the Lord your God." He could not say "against the Lord *my* God." You who can, upon Scripture grounds, lay claim to God as your God, as having a special propriety in Him, you have an interest in the covenant of grace.

Second, for God to be your God notes an all-sufficiency in God, put out for your good. In Genesis 17:1 God says to Abraham, "I am the Almighty God; walk before Me, and be thou perfect." If you can look upon God as having an interest and propriety in God; if you find by experience that God is exceedingly good to your souls in everything; if you see the emptiness of all things in the world, and that they are but particular helps to you, such as food against hunger, drink against thirst, clothes against nakedness, but you find God to be an all-sufficient help and remedy, the chief good, sufficing, satisfying, and filling your heart; if you can look upon God as your all-sufficient good, as having your portion and interest in Him and in none else, this is an undoubted evidence that you belong to the covenant of grace.

Third, for God to be your God notes God's sovereignty and power over you for your benefit: the Lord will reign over you, subdue corruptions in you, quell your pride, humble your heart, and give you a meek and quiet spirit. If you find that God is yours in these three particulars, you may comfort your heart in an unquestionable interest in the covenant of grace. If God is your God and you are His people, you have given up and devoted yourselves wholly to the service of God in everything that you do.

2. Another special blessing of the covenant of grace is that God has promised to sanctify and renew your natures. In Ezekiel 36:26–27 God says, "A new heart also will I give you, and a new spirit will I put within you, and I will take away the stony hearts out of your flesh, and will give you an heart of flesh, and I will put My Spirit within you, and cause you to walk in My statutes, and ye shall keep My

judgments and do them." God will not only give us life for
our happiness, but grace for our holiness. He will not only
give us imputed righteousness for our justification, but
also inherent righteousness for our sanctification. Now
therefore examine yourselves. Have your natures ever
been sanctified and regenerated? Have you ever been
washed with clean water, and those stains of sin and corruption wiped away from you? Has the broom of sanctification ever swept your inward man, and made it not a cave
for every unclean bird to lie in, but a habitation fit for the
Holy ghost to dwell in? If it is so, you have a real right to,
and interest in, the covenant of grace; for no man can
have the blessings of the covenant but he must have a being in the covenant of grace. It is very observable that God
is not only, as the covenant represents Him, "a God gracious and merciful, slow to anger, and full of compassion,"
but He is a holy God as well as a merciful God. Therefore
He will work holiness in us, and expect holiness from us, if
ever we expect to have mercy and happiness from Him.
Never lay claim to God, nor expect life and happiness
from Him as He is a merciful God, unless you resolve to
be conformable to Him as He is a holy God.

OBJECTION. But here some may say, "This is not as
great a blessing as you speak of, to be sanctified by virtue
of the covenant of grace; for there are many men who
may be sanctified by the covenant of grace, and yet never
be saved by it." And this objection they ground upon Hebrews 10:29: "And [he] hath counted the blood of the
covenant, wherewith he was sanctified, an unholy thing."

ANSWER. The sanctification here spoken of is not a
true sanctification, but only in profession—in the sight of
men, not in the sight of God. It is not a sanctification in
deed and in truth, but only in show and in the judgment
of men.

3. Another blessing of the covenant of grace is the forgiveness of our sin. Jeremiah 31:34: "They shall all know
Me from the least of them to the greatest of them, saith
the Lord, for I will forgive their iniquity, and will remember their sin no more." Now, beloved, can you say

that God has pardoned your sins and done away your offenses? If so, then you are under the covenant of grace.

OBJECTION. But here some poor soul may say, "Alas, I have been a great sinner, and have committed offenses against God; and therefore, I fear I have no real interest in the covenant of grace."

ANSWER. Do not be discouraged, for it is the glory of the covenant of grace to pardon great sins. It puts a great deal of glory upon God to pardon great sins and pass by great offenses. Amos 5:12, 15: "I know (says God) your manifold transgressions, and your mighty sins." Here are manifold and mighty sins, and yet God says, "Hate evil and love good; it may be the Lord will be gracious to you." Nay, the Lord *will* be gracious to you. Though you have manifold and mighty sins, yet it is not the greatness nor mightiness of them, but your stubbornness of heart in not coming in and closing with Jesus Christ that undoes you.

4. Another blessing of the covenant of grace is God's writing His law in our hearts so that we shall never depart from Him. Jeremiah 31:33: "I will put My law in their inward parts, and write it in their hearts; I will be their God, and they shall be My people." God will put into our hearts a suitable frame and disposition answerable to every command of God in His law, so that we shall be able to obey, observe, and keep it, and say that it is good. "Then," says God, "you shall never depart from Me." Now examine yourselves: has this effect been wrought by the Spirit of God in your hearts? Has God written the sermons you have heard, not in your books, but in your hearts? If so, these are good evidences of your interest in the covenant of grace.

The second discovery or characteristic of your having an interest in the covenant of grace is this: if you have in you the inseparable correlaries that belong to this covenant of grace. There are some things that always accompany the covenant of grace, as I shall instance in these particulars:

1. If you are a man under the covenant of grace, in

covenant with God, then you are disengaged from the league and covenant that you have made and contracted with your lusts. Whoever is in covenant with God has broken his league with his lusts. You cannot be in covenant with Christ till you fall off from your lusts and break off from sins. In Acts 3:25–26 the apostle said, "Ye are the children of the prophets, and of the covenant, which God made with our fathers; saying to Abraham, 'And in thy seed shall all the kindreds of the earth be blessed.' Unto you first God, having raised up His Son Jesus Christ, sent to bless you, in turning away everyone of you from your iniquities."

So that if you are children of the covenant, the Lord will turn every one of you from your wicked ways; and, therefore, you who are not turned from the evil of your courses, who have not broken that league you have made with death and hell, you can lay no claim to the covenant of grace. In Psalm 50:16–17, God says to the wicked: "What hast thou to do to. . .take My covenant into thy mouth, seeing thou hatest instruction, and castest my words behind thee?" You will not forsake your lusts, nor leave your sins; and therefore what have you to do to meddle with My covenant of grace? You can lay no claim to the covenant till you have cast off the old man and subdued and overcome your sins and corruptions.

2. Another consequence of the covenant of grace that will accompany you is this: you will be a people wholly devoted and given up to the service of God. Jeremiah 31:33: "I will be your God and you shall be My people." The covenant of grace is called a holy covenant in Luke 1:72, not so much because it was made by a holy God as because it was made for the holy creature. It will make them holy who enter into it, and therefore those who are in covenant with God are called a holy people. And they must be a holy people, for in 1 Corinthians 6:20 the apostle said, "Ye are bought with a price; therefore glorify God in your body, and in your spirit, which are God's." 2 Corinthians 7:1: "Having therefore these promises, dearly beloved, let us cleanse ourselves from all filthiness both of flesh and

spirit, perfecting holiness in the fear of God." Those who are in covenant with God are a holy and crucified people.

3. Another consequence is this: the man who has a share in the blessings of the covenant makes conscience to walk in the ways of the covenant. He will not only close with the promise of the covenant, but also make conscience of keeping the commands of the covenant; for the covenant of grace not only bestows blessings upon you, but requires something of you too. In Isaiah 55:3 God said, "Incline your ear, and come unto Me; hearken, and your soul shall live; and I will make an everlasting covenant with you, even the sure mercies of David." The covenant of grace is a sure and everlasting covenant, but, said God, you shall come unto Me first, and then I will make with you an everlasting covenant. God will have you obey him if ever you think to have any share in the covenant of grace. Regarding those who, let God command what He will, do what they please, this argues that they do not belong to the covenant of grace. But if the blessings of the covenant of grace are given by God to you, and the concomitants of it found with you, and, lastly, the conditions of it found in you, which is faith, the only condition of the covenant of grace, believe and be saved; if God has brought you into a believing state, so that there is not one promise in the gospel but you heartily assent unto and close with; if it is thus, then you may conclude that you belong to the covenant of grace. And thus I have done with these characters by way of trial.

Application

I have only now a word or two more by way of use, and so have done with this third part of man's misery. The use I shall make of this shall be for consolation to all those whose hearts can bear them witness that they enjoy the saving blessings of the covenant of grace: God to be their God and they to be his people; that God has sanctified and renewed your natures, and pardoned and passed by all your sins and iniquities, and has written His law in your hearts so that you do not depart from Him. If you have the concomitants of the covenant, that you are disengaged from the league and covenant you have made with sin and death and hell; if you are wholly devoted and given up to the service of God, and make conscience to walk in the ways of the covenant; if the conditions of the covenant of faith in Christ are found in you; if you are brought into a believing condition; if all these things are wrought in you, then hearken to the great happiness and benefit you enjoy by being under the covenant of grace.

You have that which is more worth than a king's ransom, nay, than all the world. You have God to be your God. You have more than was promised to Esther by King Ahasuerus, half of his kingdom. You have more than the devil promised to Christ when he carried Him to the top of the mountain and showed Him all the kingdoms of the world and the glory of them. You have more than the world, for you have God to be your God, and you have an interest in the covenant of grace, which is a bundle of promises, and includes in it all the promises of the gospel, which are all yours; and you may go and apply them to your own souls in whatsoever condition you are in.

You who are in covenant with God, labor to admire the great condescension of God, that He would be pleased to proceed with you by way of a covenant. I have read of some authors who have more wondered and stood amazed at this than at anything else in the world: that God who is the sovereign Lord of all the works of His hands, that He should not rule us and command us by a law, but deal with us by way of a covenant, for God is not bound to give us a reward, though we should serve Him all the days of our lives. God might command us, as we are His creatures, to serve and obey Him, to pray, read, hear, and walk holily and humbly before Him; and when we have done all this, yet He might say to us, "I will never give you heaven nor happiness, nor any reward at all." He might have said this to us, but He has condescended so far, as to make a bargain with us, that if we will believe in His Son

Jesus Christ, and live holily and walk uprightly before Him, then He will be our God and we shall be His people. He will write His law in our hearts, and sanctify and renew our natures, pardon and forgive all our sins, and give us heaven and happiness when we die. Oh, what an infinite condescension is this in God, and what an unspeakable bounty and free grace! He might say to us, "You are bound to serve, obey, love, and fear Me, but I am not bound to make a covenant with you, and promise you My Son, life, and salvation through Him. But, though I am not bound to it, yet I will give you My Son, heaven, and happiness. I will be your God, and you shall be My people. I will regenerate and sanctify your natures, create in you new hearts, and write my law in your inward parts. I will freely do all this for you," says God. Oh, what infinite condescension and free grace and mercy is this!

Another great happiness you enjoy under the covenant of grace is this: the Lord will pardon all the great sins you commit against Him, and accept all the weak duties and services you perform to Him. Though you commit great and mighty sins, yet the Lord is gracious and merciful and will pardon them. The covenant of grace covers great sins. As the sea can cover a mountain as well as a mole-hill, so the covenant of grace can pardon mountainous sins as well as small ones. And again, the covenant of grace accepts weak and imperfect duties, nay, those very duties that wicked men perform. Though they are more for the matter of them than ours are, yet by virtue of the covenant of grace the Lord accepts ours, and will not accept theirs. Proverbs 15:8: "The sacrifice of the wicked is an abomination to the Lord, but the prayer of the upright is His delight." A sacrifice is a great deal more costly than a prayer, and yet the Lord will accept a poor, penniless prayer coming from a godly man while He will reject a costly sacrifice from a wicked man. God will accept a cup of cold water from one in covenant with Him, when He will not accept ten thousand rivers of oil from a wicked man. He will pardon your great sins and accept your weak services. Indeed, if you were under a covenant of works, it would require

perfect obedience; but, being under a covenant of grace,
the Lord accepts sincere, though imperfect, obedience.
And thus I have done with the third part of man's misery,
being strangers to the covenant of grace.

11

An Unconverted Man Is Without Hope

"Having no hope." Ephesians 2:12

We come now to the fourth part of an unconverted man's misery (which you will think to be a very strange one): he is without hope. While these Ephesians were in a state of Gentilism, unconverted to the faith of Christ, they were without hope; and the reason of it was because they were without Christ, who is the way, the truth, and the life. There is no other way to heaven but by Jesus Christ. And seeing they were out of the way to heaven, they must be without any hopes of coming to heaven. It was the first branch of their misery, in being without Christ, that exposed and made them liable to all the rest. Because they were without Christ, therefore they were aliens to the commonwealth of Israel; therefore they were strangers to the covenant of promise, without hope, and without God in the world.

OBJECTION. But here some will be ready to say, "How can the apostle say they were without hope, when, were it not for hope, the heart would break? And therefore it is not possible they should be without hope."

ANSWER. I answer, it is true they had a hope, but it was a vain hope, an ungrounded and a deluding hope; and this kind of hope is no better than no hope at all. So the apostle might well say that they had no hope, that is, no good nor well-grounded hope for heaven; they had only a presumptuous hope, such a hope as would make them ashamed in the latter end. They had only the hope of the hypocrite who shall perish; and therefore, when the apostle says that these Ephesians, during their unregeneracy, were without hope, his meaning is that they

101

were without any well-grounded hopes for heaven. They had no Scripture grounds to bottom or build any hopes upon that God would bring them to heaven.

This is a very sad and dreadful point I am now upon in showing you this part of man's misery, being without hope. The observation I shall draw out from hence shall be this:

DOCTRINE. All men, during the state of their unregeneracy, are without any true or well-grounded hopes of heaven.

In handling this, I shall first prove it in general, and then improve it. I will first prove that an unconverted man's condition, in reference to his hopes for heaven, is just like Paul's, and those mariners who were with him in the ship sailing towards Rome, Acts 27:20, when neither sun nor stars appeared, but the wind and waves beat upon the ship, insomuch that all the hopes they had of being saved were quite taken away. So it is just your case if you are without Jesus Christ: neither sun nor star shines upon you. If Christ does not shine upon you, you are like Paul and the other mariners in the ship: all hope of your being saved is quite taken away from you. I shall confirm this truth to you by three or four demonstrations, that a wicked man is without any hope of heaven.

DEMONSTRATION 1. An unregenerate man must be without hope, because he is without Christ, who is the foundation of a Christian's hope. "Wherefore remember (says the apostle) that at that time ye were without Christ." And therefore he tells them that they were without hope. In Titus 2:13 Christ is called our hope. Christ is that person in and upon whom we are to build all our hopes for heaven, and therefore He is called our hope. And this is the meaning of that expression, "Christ in you the hope of glory" (Colossians 1:27), intimating that you cannot hope for glory but in and through Jesus Christ. That man who is a Christless man must be a hopeless man; that is the first demonstration.

DEMONSTRATION 2. A man without Christ must be without hope, because he is without a title to any promise of life and salvation, which is the only support and prop of man's hope. You would count this a very fond and vain hope for any man to hope that such a rich man would make him heir of all he has, though he never promised him one foot of land. Why, just so vain are the hopes of wicked men; but now the word of promise is like a pillar of marble to bear up the hearts of God's people. Titus 1:2: "In hope of eternal life, which God that cannot lie promised before the world began." The promises ground that man who has interest in them, to a hope of eternal life; he who is without the Lord Jesus Christ, the foundation of hope, and without the promises which is the pillar of hope, must be without all true hopes of heaven.

DEMONSTRATION 3. He cannot but be without hope because he is without faith that is the ground of hope. Hebrews 11:1: "Faith is the substance of things hoped for, the evidence of things not seen." Where no true faith is, there can be no hope, for faith is the mother and hope is the daughter. Hope is begotten by faith, and an unregenerate man must be without hope because he is without Christ the foundation of hope, the promises that are the pillars of hope, and faith the ground of hope.

DEMONSTRATION. 4. It appears that he is without hope, because when he leaves the world his hopes leave him, whereas the hope of a godly man never leaves him till it brings him to heaven. When a wicked man dies, his hopes are gone and leave him when he has most need of them; had his hopes been well-grounded hopes, they would never make him ashamed of them.

Thus you see I have only in general confirmed the point to you. I come now to speak of some more particular inquires in the prosecution of this doctrine. Beloved, lend me your thoughts a little in the handling of these five inquires:

I shall show you the nature of this hope that unconverted men are without.

I shall show you what are the characters of those men who are without any well-grounded hopes for heaven.

I shall show you the reason why (seeing the Scripture

says that a wicked man has no hope), of any men in the
world, a wicked man nourishes in his heart the greatest
hopes for heaven.

I shall show wherein lies the difference between those
who have only a presumptuous hope for heaven and those
who have a true and well-grounded hope for heaven.

Last, I shall show you the great misery of those men
who have only presumptuous hopes for heaven.

QUESTION 1. What is the nature of that hope unconverted men are without?

ANSWER. Take this plain description of it: the true
hope which wicked men are without is a well-grounded
and patient expectation for the accomplishment of all
those spiritual and eternal good things which God has
promised through Jesus Christ, and which faith believes. I
call it a well-grounded expectation to distinguish true
hope from those presumptuous hopes wicked men have. I
call it a patient hope to distinguish it from a rash hope in
wicked men. And I say it is a patient expectation and a
looking for the accomplishing of those spiritual and eternal good things which God has promised in Christ, because this is the ground of hope: it is called the hope of
glory, and the hope of eternal life, and the like. Thus you
have the nature of this hope that wicked men are without.
When the apostle says they were without hope, his meaning is that they were without any hope of those spiritual
and eternal good things that God has promised to believers through Christ.

QUESTION 2. What are the characters of those men
who have no hopes for heaven; or, if they have, it is only a
deluding and a presumptuous hope, a hope no better
than no hope at all? Nay, it would be a great deal better to
have no hope than to have a presumptuous hope, but that
I shall speak to afterward.

Now before I shall lay down these characteristics by
way of discovery, I will only premise five particular conclusions that are very necessary to prevent wicked men from
running into mistakes concerning their hopes for heaven.

1. This grace of hope may as well be counterfeited as

any other grace. There is a lively hope in a believer and a dead hope in a wicked man; there is a feigned hope as well as a true hope, a counterfeit hope as well as a good hope. And therefore it is said in Job 8:13: "The hypocrite's hope shall perish"; and Proverbs 10:28: "The expectation of the wicked shall perish."

2. Those men who have least grounds to build hopes of heaven upon yet nourish most confident hopes of heaven in their hearts. I shall give you two notable places of Scripture to prove this. In Proverbs 14:16 it says that "a wise man feareth and departeth from evil." A wise man is jealous over his own heart. What follows? But, says he, a fool, that is, a wicked man, rages and yet is confident; he runs on in wicked ways and practices without any remorse or sorrow, and yet is confident that he shall go to heaven as well as the best. A wise man fears and departs from evil, but a wicked man rages, and yet is confident. Those who have least cause to hope harbor the greatest hopes for heaven in their hearts. A similar place you have in Psalm 36:1: "The transgression of the wicked saith in his heart that there is no fear of God before his eyes," and yet the next words are, "he flattereth himself in his own eyes, until his iniquity is found to be hateful." Wicked men are very apt to have good conceits of themselves, and you shall find, ordinarily, that a poor soul who walks conscionably before God, neglects no known duty, mortifies every known lust, and walks humbly before God is full of fears, jealousies, and doubts that all things are not well between God and his soul. Yet you shall find another ungodly wretch, who gives way to all manner of sin and uncleanness, and fulfills the lusts of his flesh and of his mind, and this man is very confident of his going to heaven, and that all is well with him, while he is running headlong to hell. Here then you see the second conclusion that those men who have least grounds to build hopes of heaven upon nourish the strongest hopes for heaven in their hearts.

3. A man may live and die with very strong hopes that he shall go to heaven till he is thrown down into hell. He may have no other thoughts but that he shall go to heaven

till he is cast headlong into hell. I shall give you some plain text to prove this. Job 21:23 speaks of a wicked man: "One dieth in his full strength, being wholly at ease and quiet." A learned divine says that it is the note of a wicked man, when he lies upon his death bed, if you come to him and ask him if he has any hopes he shall go to heaven, he will answer that he has very strong hopes of it. And if you ask him whether any sins trouble him, he will tell you, "No, blessed be God, I have no sin troubling me now, nor ever did I in all my life." What, does nothing at all disquiet you? "No, I am wholly at ease and quiet." He has no sin troubling him, no misgiving thoughts but that he shall go to heaven. But when a wicked man dies, his expectation shall perish, and not till then. Now, beloved, I think this conclusion should a little startle you, and make you look about you to take heed lest you run hoodwinked to hell. I do not want you to live and die in hopes of heaven, and never think otherwise till you drop down into hell.

4. To you who lay claim to strong hopes for heaven, let me tell you this much: you are not to hope for heaven unless you can render a reason or ground of your hopes. Beloved, it is not natural for every man to hope for heaven and to be saved; and you ought not to hope for heaven unless you can give some grounds for it. The apostle says, "But sanctify the Lord God in your hearts, and be ready always to give an answer to every man that asketh you a reason of the hope that is in you, with meekness and fear." Now examine yourselves, what grounds can you give for your hopes of heaven? Have you a promise for it, one Scripture ground for it, or the witness of the Spirit for it? If not, then do not nourish any hopes of heaven in your hearts.

Thus I have laid down these four conclusions. I come now to handle the query itself:

QUESTION. What are the characteristics whereby it may be known whether you are such a one who has no hopes for heaven, or a mere deluding, an ungrounded and presumptuous hope, which is as good as no hope?

ANSWER. The hearts of all the sons of men are desperately wicked, and deceitful above all things. Man is a proud creature, and apt to have proud and high conceits of himself; and therefore I shall give you five distinguishing characters whereby you may know whether your hopes for heaven are true and well-grounded hopes or not.

1. The man who nourishes in his heart great hopes for heaven, and yet at the same time fosters and favors great lusts and sins in himself, has no true hopes for heaven. I shall give you a clear place to prove this in Deuteronomy 29:19–20: "And it come to pass, when he heareth the words of this curse, that he. bless himself in his heart, saying, I shall have peace, though I walk after the imaginations of mine heart, to add drunkenness to thirst, the Lord will not spare him, but then the anger of the Lord and his jealousy shall smoke against that man." And so, in Isaiah 57:10 the prophet says, "Thou art wearied in the greatness of thy ways, yet saidst thou not, there is no hope." It is a very strange place, as if the prophet should say to them, "You walk in a great course of sin and wickedness, and yet you flatter yourselves; you will not say there is no hope for you." You who nourish great sins and wickedness in your bosoms, and allow yourselves in the practice of great sins, you should say there is no hope for you to go to heaven, for God here charges it upon you that, notwithstanding you walk on in ways of sin, yet you say not there is no hope, but are rather very confident you shall go to heaven for all that. And so, in Psalm 36:1–2: "The transgression of the wicked saith in his heart, there is no fear of God before his eyes." And yet, says the Psalmist, he flatters himself with vain hopes of heaven. Wicked men have heaven and the hopes thereof in their eyes when they have sin in their hearts, and this shows that their hope is only a deluding and a vain hope.

2. That man has no true hope, but only a presumptuous and vain hope for heaven, who is strong in his expectations of heaven as his aim and end, but slow in his actions and endeavors after holiness as his way. He who can with Balaam desire to die the death of the righteous,

but never cares nor desires to live the life of the righteous, that man's hope is but a vain hope, as the Psalmist has it in Psalm 119:155: "Salvation is far from the wicked, for they seek not Thy statutes." And if salvation is far, the hope of salvation is as far. But why is salvation far from the wicked? Because they do not seek God's statutes. Those men who hope that salvation is near them, when they are far from seeking after God's statutes and endeavoring after holiness as the way to happiness, are far from salvation, and the hope of salvation too.

3. That man has only deluding hopes for heaven who is unwilling to have his hope tried, examined, and come to the touchstone, those who will not, as the apostle bids us, "Be ready to give to every man that asketh you a reason of the hope that is in you, with meekness and fear." Now let me ask you, what ground you can give for your hopes in heaven? Have you the testimony of God's Spirit for it, or the testimony of a good conscience, that in simplicity and godly sincerity, you have had your conversation here in this world? Have you a promise or any ground in Scripture for your hopes? If you have no ground for your hopes, and cannot endure to come to the trial or touchstone, it is an argument that you are counterfeit metal, that you have no real hopes for salvation and happiness in another world.

4. The man who builds his hopes for heaven more upon his own performances than upon God's promises, his hope is only a deluding hope. This is that sandy ground Christ speaks of in Matthew 7. To build your hopes of heaven upon any services you do, or any duties you perform is as if you should go about to build a house upon the sand. Ask a wicked man whereon he grounds his hopes for heaven; and he will tell you that he does the works of charity; he gives every man his due; he lives honestly and civilly among his neighbors; he hears and reads the Word; he prays and receives the sacraments; he does such and such good duties; and this is that which they build hopes for heaven upon. They think that Christ is espoused to them because they are bidden to the wedding

supper, for the ordinances of Christ are his marriage supper. They are ready to say with those in Luke 13:25–26: "We have eaten and drunken in thy presence. Lord, Lord, open to us." I do not deny but a man may have evidence from his graces, and from the work of God upon his heart, but the great pillar of marble that must bear up your hope must be the promise of God in Christ. He that builds his hopes for heaven only upon his own performances and good duties, his hope is a vain and deluding hope.

I do not deny but the graces of God's Spirit are real evidences of God's love to the soul. The apostle says, "By this we know that we are translated from death to life, because we love the brethren," and again, "By this we know that we are of God, because of his Spirit which he hath given us." But, I say, this is not the main pillar and ground of our hope. We should be so fervent in prayer, and diligent in the performance of holy duties, as if we expected to be saved by our duties; but when we have done all that we can, we must lay down all at the feet of Christ and conclude that our best righteousness is but as filthy rags. And when we have done all that we can do, we are unprofitable servants and must wholly and only depend upon the merits and mercies of Christ for salvation and comfort.

5. The man who thinks that there is neither difficulty in getting this grace of hope, nor efficacy in keeping it, has no true hope. You who think there is no difficulty in obtaining this grace never yet had it, for the least grace is beyond the power and capacity of any man to get of himself. You who think it an easy matter to hope for heaven never yet had a true hope, for it must be God who works this grace in us. The apostle says in Romans 15:13: "Now the God of hope fill you with all joy and peace in believing."

Those who think there is no efficacy in keeping this grace of hope have no true hope, for wherever true hope is, it has these properties with it:

Hope has a purifying virtue with it. 1 John 3:3: "Every man that hath this hope in Him purifieth himself, even as He is pure."

Hope has a pacifying property with it. It is the anchor of the soul, both sure and steadfast. Though the world and the devil troubles and disquiets you, and afflictions and temptations molest and disturb you, yet this grace of hope will quiet and pacify you. Those who hope in God shall be secure and at rest.

Hope has a painful property with it; it is never a sluggard. Where there is an impossibility hope is cut off. But that which a man hopes for, he will labor and endeavor after. As he who plows does so in hope, so the hopes of heaven will make you plow up the fallow ground of your hearts, and make you indefatigable in your labors after heaven so that you shall take a great deal of pains and use all your endeavors for it.

12

Causes of False Hopes in Wicked Men

"Having no hope." Ephesians 2:12

QUESTION. What is the reason (seeing the Scripture says that a wicked man has no hope) that, of all the men in the world, wicked men nourish the greatest hopes for heaven in their hearts?

ANSWER. In resolving this question, I shall lay down for you four false pillars or props that bear up and nourish the hopes of wicked men; and, as I name them to you, I shall show you the rottenness and deceitfulness and insufficiency of them for any man to build hopes of heaven upon.

PROP 1. The first prop that wicked men build hopes of heaven upon is because they have committed but small sins in their lifetime, and have not run out into the commission of such gross and scandalous sins in the world as other men have. Therefore they say, "Surely we have some ground to hope for heaven! It is true, we are sinners, but our sins are but ordinary, small sins and frailties; they are not sins of a double die." This is just as the Pharisee said, "Lord, I thank Thee that I am not as other men are: extortioners, unjust, adulterers, or even as this publican." Because he was not as bad as other men, he thought he had a right and title to heaven. Because men are not as bad as the worst, therefore they think themselves as good as the best. Now I shall show you the weakness and rottenness of this pillar for any man to build hopes of heaven upon, and that in the following particulars:

• You who make this a ground to build hopes for heaven upon, let me tell you this much: there are many men in the world who have kept themselves from great and crying sins, and yet remain in an unconverted state. For instance, you may see this in Paul. In Philippians 3:6 he tells us that according to the law he was blameless. There was no command of God, in the letter of it, that he was guilty of the breach of: he was no swearer, nor liar, nor stealer, nor drunkard, nor adulterer. He was guilty of no great and gross sins, yet Paul had nothing to plead for heaven for him if he had not had the righteousness of Jesus Christ.

Said the young man to Christ: "What shall I do to inherit eternal life?" Christ told him that he should not commit murder, nor commit adultery, nor steal, nor bear false witness, honor his father and mother, and love his neighbor as himself. The young man answered and said, "All these things have I kept from my youth up." Jesus looked upon him and loved him and pitied him, that such an ingenuous and blameless man as he was should yet go to hell. This man did not break the law of God in the letter of it, but yet he went away sorrowful when Christ bade him go and sell all that he had and give to the poor. "The young man went away sorrowful, for he had great possessions." Then Christ said, "How hardly shall a rich man enter into the kingdom of heaven!" So it was with the proud Pharisee who boasted himself over the poor publican; this man went away justified and not the other.

• You who make small sins a prop to build hopes of heaven upon, it may be though your sins are little and small, yet what they want in bulk and magnitude they may make up in number. Many small sins are more dangerous than one great sin, many small scars upon the heart with a penknife are as bad as a thrust with a sword. It may be with you in this regard as it is in arithmetic: many small figures amount to a greater sum than a few great figures do. Four small figures make a greater sum than three great figures; so many small sins will do you more harm than a few great sins. If what your sins want in bulk and magnitude you make up in number and multitude, you are as liable to damnation as if you had committed great and crying sins. Though you have not committed adultery in your life, yet, it may be, you have had many sinful and unclean thoughts in your heart. Though you have not been guilty of murder, yet maybe you have had many revengeful thoughts in you, which is as bad as murder, and so of any other sins.

• You who plead exemption and freedom from great sins to be a prop to build hopes for heaven upon, know this: small sins are more capable of great aggravations than great sins are, as I shall show you in these three particulars wherein small sins admit of greater aggravations than great sins.

First, small sins are committed most commonly, with more complacence and less reluctance than great sins. Unclean thoughts please the heart, tickle the fancy, content the mind of a man, and are committed with a great deal more complacence and delight and less reluctance. Who would strain at a gnat? Now it lays upon your souls more guilt, when you commit the smallest sins with delight and contentment, and satisfaction, than if you committed great and gross sins, if you labor to resist them, and strive against them.

Second, you commit small sins with more security and less penitence than great sins. When a man commits a great and scandalous sin, he is sensible of what he has done, and lays it to heart and is ashamed of it and must repent of it, or else it will be a shame to him all his life long. But he can venture upon a small sin and never be troubled at it nor grieved for it. He can commit a small sin with a great deal of security and impenitence, so that hereby they do the soul more wrong than great sins.

Third, you are apt to run into small sins with more frequency than you commit great sins, for they are so open to the reproof of the world, and so obvious to the eyes of all men, that you cannot find opportunities to commit them so often; whereas small sins you commit again and again, and one day after another, and a thousand times in one day, and yet never take notice of them. Therefore, this may convince you that your exemption from great sins can be no sufficient ground to build your hopes for hopes for heaven upon.

• You who build your hopes for heaven upon this ground—because your sins are none of the greatest—let me tell you that the smallest sins that you ever committed in all your lifetime, without repentance on your part and satisfaction on Christ's part, will forever keep your soul out of heaven. If you repent, peradventure you shall be pardoned; the smallest sins cannot be forgiven without the blood of Christ to wash them away. For "without the shedding of blood there is no remission of sins." And thus I have shown the insufficiency and deceitfulness of the first prop that wicked men build their hopes for heaven upon. We come now to the second.

PROP 2. "But," says a wicked man, "I have heard and read of those who have committed far greater and more crying sins than ever I have been guilty of; yet they hoped for heaven, and are gone to heaven! May not I hope as well as they? I read of David's adultery, of Noah's drunkenness, Paul's persecuting Christ, Peter's denial of Him, and divers others; and yet those men are gone to heaven. Why may not I go as well as they?"

Concerning this plea of wicked men, I shall give you these three things by way of answer:

First, you who make this a ground for your hope pervert the end for which God has recorded the examples of His servants in Scripture, for God did not record them there to be a provocation to you to go on presumptuously sinning against Him, but merely to be a restraint and caveat to keep you from falling into the same sins which they did. If Noah, Lot, David, and Peter, such holy and excellent men as these, had their failings, and committed great and gross sins, oh, then, let me take heed lest I am overtaken and fall into the same sins! This is the use that we should make of the failings of other men. 1 Corinthians 10:11: "All these things happened unto them for our examples, and they are written for our admonition, upon whom the ends of the world are come." And in 1 Timothy 1:16 the apostle says, "I obtained mercy, that in me first Jesus Christ might show forth all longsuffering, for a pattern to them which should hereafter believe on him to life everlasting."

Second, you who make the sins of other men who have obtained mercy to be a ground to build your hopes of heaven upon, let me ask you this question: you who fall into the same sins with Noah, David, or Peter, do you repent with them too? It is true, Noah did fall once into the sin of drunkenness, but the Scripture records that he was an upright man in his generation. Though David once defiled his bed, yet afterwards he repented of it, and made his couch to swim with tears for it. After Peter had denied Christ, he went out and wept bitterly for it. But, I say, what is all this to you, who makes a trade of sin, and falls into gross sins every day, time after time, and yet never mourns and grieves for them, as David did for his sin, nor weep bitterly for them with Peter. What plea can this be to encourage you to hope for heaven?

Third, know further that a godly man may fall into the same sins that others fall into, for the matter of them, but not for the manner. It is the *manner* of falling into sin, and not the matter of it that damns a man. It is true, Noah fell into the sin of drunkenness, but I shall distinguish Noah from any wicked drunkard in the world, and that in these five particular considerations:

Noah was drunk, but it was before he knew that wine would make him drunk. If you read the story, you shall find that there was never any wine drunk till that time, for Noah then began to be a husbandman and planted a vineyard. But now there is never a one of you but very well know that wine, and strong beer and the like, will intoxicate you. Yet you will not refrain from excess in drinking; there is a great deal of difference between you and Noah.

Noah was drunk, but he did not proclaim his drunkenness. The text says "He went into his tent and slept." He was ashamed of what he had done, but you proclaim your sin, and curse and swear and commit many other sins in your drunkenness.

It is true, Noah was drunk, but you never read that he was drunk any more than once. You are drunk again and again, one day after another.

Though he once fell into this sin, yet, for the ordinary course and practice of his life, he was an upright man in his generation, whereas it may be that your ordinary and frequent practice is drunkenness.

Noah was an aged man, and in this regard his age might call for more wine and strong liquor to cheer up his spirits than young people want. So that all these considerations a little mitigate and allay Noah's fault, though it is not wholly excusable.

And so likewise David committed the sin of adultery. He wallowed in an unclean bed, but yet his sin likewise may admit of some extenuation and excuse. When David came up to the housetop, he little dreamed to have seen a naked woman there, which was a very great temptation to him; but, it may be, some of you seek occasion, and contrive and plot how you may commit such a sin.

David fell into the sin but once. You shall commonly find that godly men fall into great sins but once; they take warning by the first transgression, and seldom fall into the same sin again. But now, it may be, you live in unclean thoughts and actions all your life long, and therefore this can be no prop for your hopes.

Though David fell into this sin, yet he did not continue in it long, for it was but nine months between Nathan the prophet's coming to David, and telling and reproving him for his sin, and the time that he fell into it. But, alas, some of you, it may be, are adulterers of nine years standing. There are many among us who are old adulterers, and yet never had a melting and sorrowful heart for their sins, who never wept as David did, nor mourn as he mourned.

And so Peter fell into a sin of denying his Lord and Master, but he was resolved, and verily purposed before to have confessed and not to have denied Him; and yet, when the damsel came to him and told him that he was one of those who were with Christ, Peter may have thought that they would have put him to death and crucified him as well as Christ. Upon this sudden surprise (which was a very great temptation to him) he denied Christ.

Though he denied Him thrice, yet afterwards he confessed Him as often as he denied Him; for when Christ asked him, "Simon Peter, lovest thou Me," he answered Christ three times: "Lord, Thou knowest that I love Thee."

Peter denied Christ, but afterward he went out and wept bitterly for it; and therefore, his obtaining mercy can be no ground for your hopes, who never yet repented of any of the sins you have committed.

And thus you see that the falling of these three godly men into great sins can be no prop to bear up your hopes for heaven.

I shall now show you more particularly that though the godly fall into sin, yea, even the same sins for the matter of them as you do, yet they do not fall into the same manner.

If a godly man falls into sin, it is unwittingly and unawares. In Galatians 6:1, the apostle says, "If any man be overtaken with a fault." A godly man runs away with all the speed he can from a sin and temptation, but sometimes it overtakes him against his will. But a wicked man runs after sin and overtakes it. He sins with set purpose of heart. "He plots mischief upon his bed, and sets himself in a way that is not good."

A godly man falls into sin sometimes, but it is with reluctance and opposition. The Spirit strives against the flesh; there is an opposing and striving against sin. They are not like cowards, but will fight as long as they can hold their weapon in their hands; but wicked men commit sin with greediness, with delight and complacency, without any reluctance at all.

Every sin that a godly man commits makes him more careful and watchful for the time to come. Thus it was with David in Psalm 38. Compare the title of it with Psalm 39:1. Psalm 38 is called "A Psalm of David to bring to remembrance." The subject matter of this Psalm was to bring David's sin to his remembrance, and, having spent this in remembering his sins, in the first words of the next

Psalm he says, "I said, I will take heed to my ways, that I sin not with my tongue." After he had called to remembrance his sins past, then he resolved with himself to strive against them in time to come. A godly man never falls into a sin but once, but he fears to fall into the same sin ever after.

Though a godly man falls into sin sometimes, yet he will at length get the upper hand of sin. Though for the present he is able to grapple with sin, yet he will overcome it at last. Grace will outgrow sin and get the victory over it. And thus I have shown you the second prop that wicked man build their hopes for heaven upon.

PROP 3. If you beat them off from the two former ones, then they fly to the mercies of God. "Oh," say they, "God is a very merciful God, and I hope He who made me will save me, and that I shall go to heaven as well as other men." Now I do not deny but the mercies of God are the chief prop under heaven that a man can build his hopes from heaven upon, but here I shall show you the rottenness of this prop in four regards, and that the mercies of God in general are no sufficient ground at all to build thy hopes for heaven upon, unless you can lay claim to the mercies of God in particular. For if you build your hopes upon the mercies of God in general:

The devils and damned spirits may then hope as well as you.

The common and outward mercies of God can be no good prop to build hopes for heaven upon unless you can lay claim to the saving and distinguishing mercies of God. The common outward mercies of God wicked men may have, for God is good to all, and His tender mercy is over all His works. The devils share in the common mercies of God as well as others; but these general mercies of God are no prop to build hopes for heaven upon unless you can build upon the saving and distinguishing mercies of God. David prayed: "Show mercy unto me, O God, with the mercy which Thou bearest to Thy own children." It must be electing, redeeming, sanctifying, and saving mercies that you must build your hopes for heaven upon.

The general mercies of God can be no ground of your

hopes unless you have an interest in Jesus Christ: for God is clothed with greatness, terror, dread, and wrath if you are without Jesus Christ. There were two laws God made concerning the mercy-seat.

First, the high priest was not, upon pain of death, to come to the mercy-seat unless he brought incense with him. Now what does this signify to us? Why, it represents the intercession of Christ, that as Aaron was not to come to the mercy-seat without incense, so neither can we go to the throne of grace to beg mercy from God, with any hope of audience or acceptance, unless we carry incense with us, which is the Lord Jesus Christ to plead for us.

Second, Aaron was to sprinkle the mercy-seat with blood, which typifies to us that we are not to expect mercy from God unless we have an interest in the blood of Christ.

PROP 4. To you who build your hopes for heaven upon the mercies of God in general, let me tell you that God is not prodigal of His special mercies, so as to bestow them upon all the world, but only upon a select number of men. He will have mercy only on those who fear Him. As for the wicked, those who run on in their sins, the Lord says Himself that, though He has made them, yet He will have no mercy on them. The mercies of God in general are not sufficient props to build hopes for heaven upon.

OBJECTION. But here think I hear some people ready to object against me and say, "What, do you go about to beat us off from our hopes of heaven? Would you bereave us of our hopes and drive us to despair?"

ANSWER 1. All you who have good and well-grounded hopes for heaven, I would not for all the world stagger your hopes; but as the great winds commonly root up and blow down the smaller shrubs, but settle and root the stronger oaks the faster into the ground so I would have all I have said this day, concerning the vain and deceitful hopes of wicked men, to confirm and establish your hopes and make them grow stronger and stronger.

ANSWER 2. God forbid that this should be in my heart, to drive any of you to despair; do not think that my aim in what has been said is to make any of you fall into desperation, but to keep you up and prevent you from falling into presumption, which is the more dangerous error of the two. Where the rock of desperation has split thousands, the rock of presumption has split its ten thousands.

ANSWER 3. My intention in what has been said is not to make you cast away all your hopes from heaven, only your false and ill-grounded hopes. I would have you to pull down all your tottering hopes and build them upon a more sure foundation, Jesus Christ Himself being the chief Cornerstone.

13

Further False Hopes for Heaven

"Having no hope." Ephesians 2:12

We come now to inquire further why wicked men nourish in their hearts most hopes for heaven, seeing the Scripture says they have none. The last time I answered this question by naming four false props they build hopes for heaven upon. I shall now give you four more.

PROP 5. Another false prop that wicked men build hopes for heaven upon is their frequency in the performance of religious duties. Thus they reason with themselves: "Shall I use duties all the days of my life as my way to heaven, and shall I not hope for heaven at my journey's end?" Though a wicked man notionally hopes for heaven through Christ, yet he lays the chief foundation of his hopes in his own good works. Christ said that in the last day men shall come to Him and cry, "Lord, Lord, open to us, for we have prophesied in Thy name, and eaten and drunk in Thy presence. We have heard Thy word, and done many miracles, and cast out devils in Thy name." They shall boast of their hearing, praying, and good works, and make that a plea for heaven; while Christ shall say unto them, "Depart from Me, I know you not."

Now I shall show you the rottenness and insufficiency of this prop to build hopes for heaven upon; but I would not have you mistake me, as if I went about to beat down good works and make duties useless. For I would have you perform duties as if you were to be saved by duties, but, when you have done all that you can do, to lay them down at the feet of Christ and wholly depend upon Him, as if we had done no duties at all. But if you make the bare performance of duties to be a prop for your hopes of heaven, it will be a very rotten and deceitful prop, as I shall show you in these four particulars:

First, all performance of duties not rendered to God the Father by Jesus Christ will be rejected by Him. Were it possible for you to kneel so long in prayer to God that you wore out your knees; were it possible for you to cry out your eyes with weeping, and by mourning and lamenting for your sins to dry up all the moisture of your body; were it possible for you to spend all the days of your life in hearing, reading, praying, and performing holy duties, yet if you do not offer them up to God in the name and mediation of Jesus Christ, they are all but like numbers that amount to no sum at all unless the righteousness of Christ is added to them. It is Christ's righteousness that makes our services acceptable to God. Christ adds His incense to the prayers of all His saints. Now, beloved, though you make never so many prayers, yet if you have no share in Christ, nor in His sufferings, prayers, and intercessions to God for you, all your prayers and holy duties are worth nothing. They will never bring you to heaven. Our persons must be in Christ before our services can be accepted by God; and therefore the bare performance of duties can be no prop to you for to build hopes for heaven upon.

Second, these things can be no prop of your hopes for heaven because hypocrites, whose persons and performances God hates, are frequent in duties as well as you. The Pharisees fasted twice a week, gave alms, and performed holy duties. So did those spoken of in Isaiah: "They did delight to draw near to God, and to know his ways, as a nation that did righteousness, and forsook not the ordinances of God; wherefore have we fasted, say they, and Thou seest not?" God did not accept anything they did. Those in Zechariah kept four fasting days a year for seven years together, and yet they said He did not regard them. Likewise, God does not regard the prayer of the wicked, as in Proverbs 15:8: "The sacrifice of the wicked is an abomination to the Lord." So is their hearing then, for they come to hear when their hearts are after their covetousness.

Third, know this much: those very duties which God accepts at the hands of His children, those very duties will He reject at the hands of wicked men. And therefore the bare performance of duty can be no prop to build hopes for heaven upon. Though you spend more time in prayer, and more time in hearing, reading, and fasting than a godly man does, yet the Lord will accept his duties and not yours. I shall give you three instances for this. The first is Cain and Abel. Abel offered the first of his sheep and cattle, the first of his flock, and Cain offered the first fruits of his ground. Now by faith Abel offered a more excellent offering than Cain. Though Cain's offering was of more value than Abel's was, yet Abel's was accepted while the other's was not. Abel's sacrifice was accepted not in regard of the quantity and worth and value of it, but because Abel was a believer, a justified man in the sight of God, and therefore he had respect first to his person and then to his sacrifice. Another instance is in 1 Kings 18. Elijah the prophet took two bullocks, and bid the prophets of Baal to choose one, and you must think they would not choose the worst of them, and he took the other. Yet the Lord showed a token of acceptance to Elijah and his sacrifice, though it was the worst of the bullocks, and showed no acceptance to the prophets of Baal. And the reason was because Elijah was a justified man in the sight of God, while the others were not. In Proverbs 15:8 it says that "the sacrifice of the wicked is an abomination to the Lord, but the prayer of the upright is His delight." God delights in a poor, penniless prayer coming from a godly man, while He will not accept a costly sacrifice coming from a wicked man.

Fourth, the bare performance of duties can be no prop to build hopes for heaven upon, because God does not look so much upon the matter of the duties you perform as upon the manner, how, and the end, why. Though you perform duties, for the matter of them, as God requires and commands, yet if they are not done in a right manner, God looks upon it as nothing. God will not own those duties as being done to Him that are not done in a right manner and to a right end. John 16:24: "Hitherto (said Christ) have ye asked nothing in My name; ask and ye shall receive, that your joy may be full." They had put up many petitions in His name, but because they did not do it in a right manner, Christ looked upon it as if they had asked nothing at all.

PROP 6. Another false prop that wicked men build hopes of heaven upon is a mere mistake of the promises and pillar of hope in Scripture, and this is done two ways: either they make those promises to be props of hope which are not, or they misapply those promises that are true grounds of hope.

They make those to be props of hope that are not. I shall name you three of them. The first is that passage in our common liturgy: "At whatever time a sinner repents from the bottom of his heart, I will blot out all his sins out of my remembrance, saith the Lord." This very sentence has been a means to delude a world of men, whereas, indeed, it is no ground at all to build hopes for heaven upon. There are no such words as these to be found in the whole Scripture. The only place where these words are found is in the common liturgy, which liturgy is but an abstract of the popish mass; for though all that is in the popish mass is not in the Book of Common Prayer, yet all that is in the Book of Common Prayer is in the popish mass. Perhaps you will scarcely believe this, but it is true, as you may see if you look into the second volume of the *Book of Martyrs*, where there is a letter inserted of King Edward VI, sent to the papists in Cornwall who were risen up in arms about the translating of the mass into English. They would by no means agree to this, but rose up to oppose it. King Edward, to pacify them, wrote to them on this matter: "As for the Service book, the translating of it may seem to you to be some new thing, but they are the very same words in English which were before in Latin, and if the mass-book which is in Latin is good, then it is as good now, though it is translated into English."

You will say, "The Lord Himself said these words, 'At whatever time a sinner repents, I will blot all his sins out of My remembrance, saith the Lord.' " I answer, it is not said so in the whole book of God, and if you look into that text of Scripture which they ground their contention that the Lord said so, you shall find it otherwise. It is in Ezekiel 18:21. Mark these words, for they are God's words indeed: "If the wicked will turn from all his sins that he hath committed, and keep all My statutes, and do that which is lawful and right, he shall surely live, he shall not die." They say if a wicked man repents of his sins. Now repentance is a general work. Judas repented, but his repentance did him no good. But here you see it is said that "If a wicked man turn from all his evil ways, and do that which is lawful and right, then he shall surely live."

A second Scripture prop that wicked men build their hopes for heaven upon, but is indeed no prop, is that "The righteous man sinneth seven times a day." This is one of the greatest props a wicked man has. He says, "What, do you tell me of my sins? The best men have their failings. The righteous sin seven times a day, and why may I not go to heaven as well as they?" Wicked men make this a great prop to their hopes, when indeed there is no place of Scripture like this in the whole Bible. That which comes nearest to it is Proverbs 24:16: "A just man falleth seven times and riseth up again, but the wicked shall fall into mischief." Now there is no mention of falling into sin in the text, nor any mention of a day, only this: "A just man falleth seven times, and riseth again." St. Augustine gives this sense of the word: "A godly man falls seven times, that is, oftentimes," expounding this place with that in Job 5:19, "He shall deliver thee in six troubles, and in seven there shall no evil touch thee." A righteous man, says Augustine, falls seven times, not sins seven times. He does not fall into sin, but into affliction. The righteous falls seven times, that is, the godly in this world are liable to fall seven times into affliction, that is, very often into afflictions and troubles while he lives here in this world. According to Job it is: "In six troubles and in seven the Lord shall deliver thee," meaning oftentimes. And therefore this place carries no reference at all of falling into sin seven times a day.

Suppose it were so, that the righteous did sin seven times a day, yet the text says in the next words, "That as often as he falleth he riseth again." Now it may be that many of you who make this a prop for your hopes of heaven fall into sin day after day, and yet never rise out of them again by repentance. You leave out the words "and riseth again." Many of you live your whole lives in an evil course: you wallow and lie down in sin, and therefore this can be no prop for your hopes.

A third sentence that they make a Scripture prop, but is not, is this: Christ died for all men, and for every man in the world. This comes within the Arminian bounds, but this opinion is taken up by others as well, who hold to universal redemption; but because I have already preached two or three sermons upon this subject, I shall therefore only now speak as much as is needful to show you the rottenness and insufficiency of this prop. Suppose that Christ did die for all, yet those men who are of this opinion do not hold that all men are saved by Christ. Some men may fall off from Christ and be damned, not withstanding the fact that Christ died for them. Take this by way of answer, it is not likely that they should have benefit by Christ's blood who have no benefit by His death.

To you who make this a plea for your hopes of heaven, observe this: these general expressions are very ill understood if you say they speak of universal and general redemption. 2 Corinthians 5:14–15: "Because we thus judge, that if one died for all, then are all dead, and he died for all, that they which live should not henceforth live unto themselves, but unto Him which died for them, and rose again." Here none can lay claim to Christ's death but those who live for Christ who died for them. And in Hebrews 2:9: "But we see Jesus who was made a little lower than the angels, for the suffering of death, crowned with glory and honor, that He by the grace of God should taste death for every man." But mark the restraint in the next words: "For it became Him for whom are all things, and by whom are all things, in bringing many sons unto glory (here the apostle restrains the words) to make the Captain of their salvation perfect through sufferings; for both He that sanctifieth, and they who are sanctified are all one, for which cause He is not ashamed to call them brethren." The apostle once again restrains the words, and therefore this can be no more a prop for your hopes who are not sanctified. But this may suffice for the first branch, in showing you how wicked men make those places to be Scripture props for their hopes that are not.

If they do not make those places to be Scripture props that are not, yet they misapply those places that indeed are Scripture promises and grounds of hope. One example is this: "Christ came into the world to save sinners." Now this is a Scripture promise, for Christ came to "seek and save them that were lost." But now, beloved, men misapply this general pillar of hope. They take the general notions of them, and this makes an abundance of people harbor great hopes of heaven in their hearts. But I shall show you wherein they misapply them.

They misapply them by not considering that a man must be first in Christ before he can lay claim to any promise of Christ. They run to the promise, but never examine first whether or not they have an interest in Christ. The promise is good and comfortable, but it cannot convey any comfort to your soul unless you are in Jesus Christ, any more than a dry pipe can convey water to you without the fountain. We are first made Christ's, and then we have a right and title to all the promises of God in Christ. If you have an interest in Christ, you have all the promises, as it were, bound up in a bundle, which you may have recourse to, and make use of when you will.

They misapply them when they object and say that the promises run in free and general terms having no conditions annexed to them.

It is true, there are some promises that are absolute so as to have no condition going before them, but *every* promise in the gospel has some condition or other annexed to it. If it has no condition going before it as meritorious, yet it has a condition that follows after it, such as in Genesis 17:1: "I am the Almighty God; (what then?) walk before Me and be thou perfect." 2 Corinthians 6:16–18: "I will be their God, and they shall be My people. . . And I will be a Father unto you, and ye shall be My sons and daughters, saith the Lord God Almighty." What follows? In the first verse of the next chapter the apostle says, "Having therefore these promises, dearly beloved, let us cleanse ourselves from all filthiness both of the flesh and spirit, perfecting holiness in the fear of God." 1 Timothy 1:15 says that "Christ Jesus came into the world to save sinners," but there is a condition after it that we find in Hebrews 2:11: "He that sanctifieth, and they who are sanctified, are all of one." There is no promise in all the gospel that does not have a condition prefixed or annexed to it. In Matthew 11:28 Christ says, "Come unto Me, all ye that labor and are heavy laden, and I will give you rest." There is a foregoing condition: we must come to Christ. There are other promises that have conditions going after. I could instance divers, but these shall suffice.

There are two props more; they are but very short ones. I shall go over one of them now, because I would not be hindered in my afternoon's work in showing you the difference between those who have a real and well-grounded hope, and those who have only a false and deluding hope.

PROP 7. Another false prop that wicked men build hopes for heaven on is this: because they live honestly and justly among their neighbors. They give every man his due, and do nobody any wrong, and therefore they conclude themselves in a very good condition.

Were this a sufficient ground for hope for heaven, there would be more heathens going to heaven than you; for they walk very exactly, and are just and upright in all their dealings. But wicked and bad men may have very good meanings in them, as we may see in the case of Balaam. In Numbers 23:10 he desired to "die the death of the righteous," that his last end might be like his. This was a good desire and meaning in him.

Though a bad meaning will defile and pollute a good action, yet a good meaning cannot advantage nor do a bad action any good. The Scribes and Pharisees performed very good actions in themselves, but they had self-ends and bad meanings that spoiled all their duties. Good meanings cannot justify bad actions. If your actions are wicked, good meaning can do you no good. In Romans 3, those who say "Let us do evil that good may come," their damnation is just.

Let your meaning be never so good, yet if you have an ignorant mind it is worth nothing. Proverbs 19:2: "The soul without knowledge, it is not good." As no man ever became rich by meaning and purposing to be rich, but by laboring and endeavoring after it, so no man ever went to heaven by good meanings without good actions accompanying them.

OBJECTION. But, say they, we do nobody any harm, but pay every man his own.

ANSWER 1. Though you pay every man his own, yet do you give God His own? Or, rather, do you not wrong God and do Him infinite indignities?

ANSWER 2. Though you do no man wrong, yet do you not wrong your own souls? We use to say of free-hearted men, "They are enemies to no man but themselves." So now do not you do your own souls wrong by harboring bosom lusts and corruptions in your souls? What benefit will it be to you that you do nobody else wrong when you do your own souls wrong? You are no better than the Pharisees, for they were very exact in giving every man his due. The proud Pharisee could boast in Luke 18:11: "I am no extortioner, nor unjust man." You may mean well and give every man his due, and yet be a wicked man.

14

Well-Grounded Hopes for Heaven

"Having no hope." Ephesians 2:12

PROP 8. We come now to the last prop that wicked men build their hopes of heaven upon. If you beat them off from all the former props, from their small sins, from the mercies of God in general, from their good duties, and good meanings, then they run to this last plea: "Have we not reason to nourish hopes for heaven? For we have been present with dying men who have been as bad as we in their lifetime, and yet they have had very strong hopes for heaven and strong hopes in God. You know that dying men will speak the truth, and therefore why may we not nourish hopes for heaven as well as they?"

This is a very strong prop wicked men build their hopes upon, but I shall show you the rottenness and insufficiency of it in these five particulars.

First, you must know that it is one thing to die stupidly and another thing to die hopefully and peaceably. Indeed, the worst men in the world may die stupidly. Their consciences may not do its office when they die. They may have their consciences seared, as it were, with a hot iron, and think they are going to heaven, and never think otherwise till they drop down into hell. But the godly die full of peace and comfort. Psalm 37:37: "Mark the perfect man, and behold the upright, for the end of that man is peace." But "there is no peace, saith my God, to the wicked," Isaiah 57:21. There may be a searedness of conscience and stupidity of heart, but they cannot die peaceably and in hope.

Second, you who, because you have seen wicked men die peaceably like lambs, let me tell you that it is the

130

greatest judgment in the world for a wicked man to die peaceably and quietly, in delusions and conceits of going to heaven, while they are tumbling headlong to hell. It would be better for him if God let the flashings of hellfire fly in his face; it would be better for him if his conscience told him his danger and his doom of dying in a stupid manner. In Job 21:23 it is said that a wicked man "dies in his full strength, being wholly at ease and quiet." No sin troubles him; no danger makes him afraid. Psalm 73:4–5: "There are no bands in their death, but their strength is firm. They are not in trouble as other men, neither are they plagued like other men." They have no trouble in their lifetime and no bands in their death. Now this is to be looked upon as a judgment upon them, not a mercy.

Third, if this peace and quietness in a wicked man's conscience arises from any grounded assurance or hope of heaven, then it might be looked upon as a blessing; but, when it arises merely from the delusions of his own heart, then it is nothing but, as it were, a golden door to let him into hell. It shall be with him as is said in Isaiah 29:8: "An hungry man dreameth, and behold, he eateth: but he awaketh, and his soul is empty." So a wicked man dreams he is going to heaven when he is falling down into hell.

Fourth, there may be great hopes of heaven expressed in a dying man's words when there is not so much peace and quietness in his heart. Proverbs 14:13: "Even in laughter, the heart is sorrowful." In the midst of a wicked man's boasting, there is a fear of hell.

Fifth, though you have seen some men who have died with stupidity of heart and depart quietly, yet there are other wicked men whose consciences are awakened, who die full of horror and terror and amazement. When their consciences tell them that they have died swearers, liars, drunkards, or adulterers, they are filled with horror and terror of conscience. Though he thought all his lifetime he would go to heaven, yet he now fears he is going down into hell.

And thus I have done with the third question, in showing you the reason why, (seeing the Scripture says that a

wicked man has no hope) that of all the men in the world,
wicked men nourish the greatest hopes for heaven in their
hearts. There are only two questions more to handle, and
then I will come to the fifth branch of man's misery.

QUESTION 4. Seeing the Scripture says that a wicked
man has no hope, and esteems their false and presumptuous hope to be as good as no hope, then how shall we
know the difference between those well-grounded hopes a
godly man has and those presumptuous and deluding
hopes wicked men have?

ANSWER. I shall here give you six apparent differ-
ences between them.

1. The hopes of a godly and regenerate man for
heaven are gotten by, and grounded upon, the Word of
God. Therefore it is called the hope of the gospel, because it is gotten by the gospel as the means, and
grounded upon the gospel as the end. That we (says the
apostle) "through the comfort of the Scriptures might
have hope." A godly man has his comforts from the Scriptures. Psalm 119:49: "Remember the word unto Thy servant, upon which Thou hast caused me to hope." But the
hopes of wicked men, as they are gotten they know not
how, so neither do they know upon what they are
grounded. And this is the reason why they are called presumptuous hopes, for this is presumption: when a man
believes a thing when he can have no visible nor likely
means to ground or bottom his hopes upon.

2. True and patient hope is bottomed upon the mercies of God and the merits of Jesus Christ. And hence
Christ is called our hope because He is the foundation on
whom believers build all their hopes for heaven. Likewise
they build their hopes on the mercies of God. Psalm
147:11: "The Lord taketh pleasure in them that fear Him,
in those that hope in His mercy." And again in Psalm
33:18: "The eye of the Lord is upon them that fear Him,
upon them that hope in His mercy." And in Psalm 52:8
David says, "I trust in the mercy of God for ever and ever."
A godly man is cast out of himself, and out of an opinion
of his own righteousness. His hopes are only built upon

the mercy of God and the merits of Christ. But the false and presumptuous hopes that wicked men have are not built so much upon God's mercy as their own duties, not so much upon the merits of Christ, what He has done for them, as upon their own duties, what they have done for themselves.

3. True hope comforts and bears up the heart under all the discomforts that it meets with in the world. David says, "I had fainted under my afflictions, but that Thy word is my hope." Hence it is that you have these two admirable expressions put together in Romans 5:2–3: "Rejoice in hope," and "glory in tribulation." These are put together to show that when a man can rejoice in hope, he can glory in all the tribulations he meets with in the world. But presumptuous hopes are like lead and ponderous weights that will make you sink under every affliction. It is only a true and saving hope that will enable you to hold up your heads under all afflictions and troubles.

4. True hope as well acts for heaven as hopes for heaven; but a presumptuous hope hopes for heaven as its end, but yet never acts holiness as its way to heaven. True hope, as it hopes for heaven, so it labors to work out its salvation with fear and trembling. You have an admirable passage for this in Psalm 119:166. David says, "Lord, I have hoped for Thy salvation, and Thy commandments." Here is both hoping and acting for heaven put together. Wicked men hope for heaven, but they do not obey God's commands. So in Psalm 37:3: "Trust in the Lord, and do good." Here is trusting and doing put together. True hope acts for heaven as well as hopes for heaven; but false hope hopes much and acts little. Wicked men will hope for salvation, but not work out their salvation; they will hope for heaven but not labor for heaven. This is the fourth difference.

5. The man who has true hope makes conscience to keep his heart pure and free both from the love of sin and the dominion of sin while he lives here in this world. You have a plain text for this in 1 John 3:3: "Every man that hath this hope in Him purifieth himself, even as He is

pure." He labors and endeavors to keep his heart upright and pure, free from sin. But a false hope will hope for heaven, though they walk on after the imaginations of their own hearts. Isaiah 57:10: "Thou art wearied in the greatness of thy way, yet saidst thou not, there is no hope." Though they had great sins, yet they had great hopes for heaven. If you are such a one as is mentioned in Deuteronomy 29:19, who says, "I shall have peace, though I walk after the imagination of mine heart, to add drunkenness to thirst"; if you are such a one, your hope is only a presumptuous hope.

6. True hope flows from a long and well-grounded experience. This is the reason for that expression in Romans 5:4: "Patience [worketh] experience, and experience, hope." True hope flows from a long and well-grounded experience in the ways of God; from an experience of the grace, bounty, and love of God to your soul; from experience of the goodness, mercy, and promises of God: and likewise from an experience of your own heart in withstanding temptations, subduing corruption, and performing holy duties. Such experiences as these are inlets to a well-grounded hope for heaven; but the hopes of wicked men are only the results of ignorance. Those who never had an experience of themselves, nor of the ways of God, have most hopes, but their hopes are only deluding and presumptuous hopes. Wicked men who so quickly get into a state of hope without any former experience of the ways of God, it is a sign that their hopes are only vain and empty hopes. They are but pithy hopes: just like your pithy trees, as elders, and withies, and such like trees, they shoot up fastest, and grow up soonest; whereas the more firm and stronger wood, such as oaks, and elm, and the like, are a great while longer in growing before they come to maturity. So it is a great while before a godly man can get a well-grounded assurance of his hopes for heaven.

Application

And thus I have done with the doctrinal part of this fourth branch of man's misery: he is without hope. We come now to the application, and the use that I shall make of it shall be threefold. There is a use of consolation, a use of terror, and a use of instruction.

USE OF CONSOLATION. This is for consolation to the people of God: though the Scripture says a wicked man has no hope, yet it says otherwise of you who are the people of God. The Scripture tells you that your hope is laid up in heaven for you and the Lord is your hope. Though wicked men have no hopes for heaven, yet you have grounded and assured and have certain hopes for heaven. Your hope is laid up for you in another world. The wicked have only their hopes in this life, and when they die, their hopes shall perish. Proverbs 11:7: "When a wicked man dieth, his expectation shall perish, and the hope of unjust men perisheth." But it is not so with you, "for the godly hope in their death." And this hope of a godly man is not as the papists hold, for though they grant that a believer has hope, yet they deny that any have assurance. They say that all a believer's evidence for heaven is only a hope, a peradventure (a most uncomfortable tenet), whereas the Scripture says there is as full an assurance of hope as of faith. In Hebrews 6:11 the apostle says, "Show all diligence to the full assurance of hope unto the end." And so in Romans 5:5: "Hope maketh not ashamed." Your hopes are not like the hopes of men who hope for dead men's shoes (as the proverb is), for they may go on barefoot before they die. But Christ, who is our hope, has died already and risen again. He has made His will and testament, and has left us legacies and bequeathed riches to us. Our hopes are well-grounded hopes, not as other men's are, who will leave them when they have most need of them.

USE OF TERROR. The second use shall be to show you the misery of those men who have only presumptuous hopes for heaven.

You are unlikely to be converted, more than any other men in the world. And this is the reason why the Scripture tells us that whores and harlots shall go to heaven before the scribes and Pharisees; yet they were a very strict people, and walked outwardly very holily. It is an easier matter to convince a harlot of her sins than to convince a proud Pharisee, who thinks himself as good as the best, and has lived in peace all his life time.

Let me tell you this much: your hopes will leave you when you have most need of them. Proverbs 11:7: "When a wicked man dieth, his expectation shall perish; and the hope of unjust men perisheth." He looks for heaven, but he shall be disappointed. Job 8:14 says that his confidence shall be cut off, and his trust shall be like a spider's web. The spider wraps himself in his web and dwells there securely all the week long, but at the end of the week, when the maid comes to sweep the windows, she sweeps down both the web and the spider. Just so the hopes of all wicked men shall come to nothing. Job 11:20: "The eyes of the wicked shall fail, and they shall not escape; and their hope shall be as the giving up of the ghost." A dying man, a little before his death, is pretty joyful and merry, and entertains some hopes of a longer life, but when his eyestrings crack, and the tokens of death appear upon him, his heart fails him, and all his hopes are dashed in pieces and taken from him. Just so it is with wicked men: they are full of hopes for heaven till they come to die, but then their hopes leave them and all their expectations perish.

Your harboring false and presumptuous hopes for heaven produces this threefold miserable and unavoidable effect upon you: frustration, vexation, and damnation.

It produces frustration and disappoints all your hopes. When you are dying, you hope that after death you shall launch forth into a sea of joy and pleasure. On the contrary, you shall launch forth into a river of brimstone, which the breath of the Lord shall kindle. You hope, it may be, that after death you shall be carried by angels into

Abraham's bosom, while you may be carried by the devils
into Beelzebub's bosom. You, it may be, hope that death
shall be a door to let you into heaven, while it shall be
only a back door to let you fall down into hell.

It shall produce in you vexation. Now vexation arises
either from disappointment or revenge. Wicked men shall
not only have a privation of happiness, but a vexation in
the loss of happiness. And hence it is that some divines
give the reason why it is said in Matthew 8:12 that in hell
"there shall be weeping and gnashing of teeth." Some are
of the opinion that, as our fire burns hot, so the fire of
hell shall burn cold, but that is but a fancy. Our divines say
that there shall be gnashing of teeth in hell, in token of
the vexation of mind that shall be in wicked men because
all their hopes are so frustrated and disappointed that
they shall gnash their teeth for vexation of mind. "When
they shall see Abraham, and Isaac, and Jacob, and all the
prophets in the kingdom of God, and they themselves
thrust out."

These false hopes will likewise produce your damnation. A wicked man who harbors false hopes for heaven in
his heart is like a man sleeping upon the mast of a ship. It
may be that he is dreaming a very pleasant and delightful
dream, and all of a sudden comes a blast of wind and
blows him into the sea. So a wicked man is but in a golden
dream on his deathbed; he hopes he is going to heaven
till he is plunged down into hell. All this represents to you
the dreadful condition of those men who have only presumptuous hopes for heaven.

USE OF INSTRUCTION. If this doctrine is true, then
this may teach us these lessons:

1. Let us take heed lest we run into this easy delusion.
There are some in the world who fall into it, and therefore why may not we as well as others? Therefore take
heed that you do not fancy to yourselves false hopes of
heaven.

2. You who are godly, take heed that you do not cast
off all your hopes for heaven. Do not say that hope is cut
off from you. As wicked men are apt to harbor groundless

hopes for heaven, so good men are too apt to cast *off* grounded hopes for heaven. Therefore do not say there is no hope for you, for there *is* hope for you.

3. Do not harbor in your hearts common and ordinary conceits of this grace of hope, as if it were so easy a matter to obtain it. It is natural for men to think that this grace of hope is very easy to be gotten, for they say, "Were it not for hope, the heart would break." Wicked men are ready to think that this grace of hope is easy to be gotten by anybody, and to be had by all. Therefore take heed of this, and consider that there is the same certainty, the same excellency, and the same efficacy in this grace of hope as there is in faith.

There is the same certainty in it. Hebrews 6:11 calls it the full assurance of hope.

There is the same excellency in it. Titus 2:13 calls it a blessed hope.

There is the same efficacy in it as there is in the grace of faith. Acts 15:9 says that faith purifies the heart. And so likewise does hope. 1 John 3:3: "Every man that hath this hope in Him purifieth himself, even as He is pure."

There is the same difficulty in getting hope as in getting faith: for this is gotten by the Word of God, Romans 10:17, and so is hope. Colossians 1:23 says that it is gotten by the preaching of the Word.

Faith is wrought in us by the power of God. Hebrews 12:2: "Jesus, the Author and Finisher of our faith." And so hope likewise is wrought in us by the power of the Holy Ghost. Romans 15:13: "that ye may abound in hope through the power of the Holy Ghost."

So hereby you see that you ought not to have such low thoughts of this grace of hope, as if it were an easy matter for every man to get it; for there is as much certainty, as much excellency, as much efficacy in this grace, and as much difficulty in getting this grace of hope as there is in faith. And thus I have done with the fourth branch of an unconverted man's misery, that he is without any well-grounded hopes for heaven.

15

Unconverted Men Are Without God in the World

"And without God in the world." Ephesians 2:12

We come now to the fifth misery of men by nature, that they are without God in the world. And here, first, I shall give you something from the order of the words, then unfold them, and then draw out some doctrines from them.

QUESTION 1. Why is their being without Christ put in the first place of the text, and their being without God put in the last place?

ANSWER. Their being without Christ is put in the first place because it was the inlet of all their misery, and their being without God is put in the last place because it is the final upshot of man's misery. It is the inlet of a man's misery to be without Christ, and it is his misery to be an alien to the commonwealth of Israel, a stranger to the covenant of promise, and to be without hope; and it is the upshot of all your misery to be without God in the world. Here I shall show you that there are multitudes of men and women in the world who are without God. Though they worship God every day, yet they may live all their days without God. But before I speak to this, I must unfold two or three things in the words.

How can it be said here that they were without God in the world when the apostle says in another place that the wicked cannot be without God? The Lord "is not far from every one of us, for in Him we live, and move, and have our being." Here the apostle says that wicked men are not far from God, and that they live in God. Therefore, how can it be said in the text that wicked men are without God in the world, whereas we are all God's offspring and come from God? How can this be?

The answer is very easy: in some sense, there is no man nor creature in the world without God; yet in another sense, there are multitudes of men who are without God in the world. In some sense there is no man who can be said to be without God, that is, by way of creation, preservation, sustentation, and ruling over us. Everyone is in God by way of creation and preservation; but in another sense there are multitudes of people without a reconciled God, without God as a father in Jesus Christ, without a God that they can lay claim to as theirs. In this sense multitudes of people are without God in the world.

Another thing that I shall explain to you is what it is to be without God, and without God in the world.

To be without God includes, in Scripture phrases, these four things:

To be without the knowledge of the true God.

To be without the true worship of the true God.

To be without a true obedience to the true God.

And to be without a peculiar interest and propriety in God.

To be without God is to be without the knowledge of the true God. A man is said to be without God when he does not know the true God. Every man in the world has something or other to be his god. In Jonah 1:5–6, when there was a great tempest upon the sea, and the ship likely to be cast away that Jonah was in, it is said that every man prayed to his god, and Jonah prayed to the Lord his God. And in Micah 4:5: "For all people will walk every one in the name of his god, and we will walk in the name of the Lord forever and ever." Every man may have something to worship as a god, and yet be without the true God. Those are said to be without God who are without the knowledge of the true God, as you may see in 2 Chronicles 15:3. It is said there that "for a long season Israel hath been without the true God." Without God, how so? Does not God rule and govern and preserve the world? Yes, but they are said to be without God because they were without the knowledge of God, for mark the next words: "they were without a teaching priest, and without law." So all the while they lay in ignorance of the true God, they were said to be without God.

Men may be said to be without God when they are without the true worship of the true God. All the while the children of Israel had the ark among them, which was the sign of God's presence, God was among them; but when the ark was taken, God was gone too. The Lord will be with you while you are with Him; while you worship God sincerely and uprightly according to His will, so long God will be with you.

To be without God is to live without true obedience to the true God. When men so live that the commands of God bear no sway over them, it is sign they are without God. Psalm 81:11: "My people, saith God, would not hearken to My voice, and Israel would none of Me." Not obeying God's commands is not having God. You are without God in the world, O man, unto whose conscience the sovereignty and authority of God cannot give a check and control to your lusts, to bring you into obedience to Him.

To be without God in the world is to be without a peculiar interest and propriety in God as your God, when you cannot say that God is your Father.

Now if you ask me in which of these four senses these Ephesians here in the text were without God, I answer that they were without God in all of them, for while they were in a state of Gentilism they were without the knowledge of the true God, without the worship of the true God, without any obedience to the true God, and without any real interest and propriety in God; but chiefly the two latter are included in this phrase.

The general point of doctrine I shall observe from this last branch of man's misery shall be this:

DOCTRINE 1. Every man, during the state of his unregeneracy, is without God in the world.

But here some may inquire what is meant by this expression, "without God in the world." The meaning is that they were without any propriety or interest in God in this world, and if they are without God in this world they must of necessity be without God in another world. And thus you have the words explained to you.

I shall now give you a more particular view of these words: "without God in the world." The words, as they are rendered in our translation, incline this way: for a man to be without any peculiar interest and propriety in God. But these words ("without God in the world") in the Greek signify "atheists in the world"; that is, they lived as if there were no God in the world. So, then, the words being thus opened, there are two things involved in this phrase "without God in the world."

1. They were atheists in the world, that is, living as if there were no God in the world.

2. They were living in the world without any peculiar interest or propriety in God.

From the first of these, that they were atheists in the world, you may note this:

DOCTRINE 2. Every man in the state of unregeneracy is an atheist in the world. He is a man who lives as if there were no God in the world. Every man in the state of unregeneracy is a practical atheist. Now when I tell you that every wicked man is an atheist, do not mistake me, for there are two sorts of atheists: an atheist in judgment and an atheist in practice. An atheist in judgment is as pagans and heathens are, but an atheist in practice lives as if there were no God in the world. So the doctrine is that every unregenerate man is a practical atheist, that is, he lives as if there were no God in the world. Psalm 14:1: "The fool hath said in his heart there is no God," that is, he lives as if there were no God who takes notice of what he does. You are a practical atheist, O man, who lives in the world as if there were no God.

And here I shall show you how it comes to pass that any man is so grossly wicked to live as if there were no God in the world, and I shall give you the characters of a man who lives after this manner.

QUESTION. How does it come to pass that men

should be so grossly wicked, such practical atheists, to live as if there were no God in the world? I shall give you four grounds of it.

1. The first reason is because of God's forbearance towards them. Ecclesiastes 8:11: "Because sentence against an evil work is not executed speedily" when they commit a sin, therefore they run into thoughts of atheism, and sin with greediness as if there were no God in the world. Psalm 50:21: "These things hast thou done, and I kept silence; thou thoughtest that I was altogether such an one as thyself." Because God held His tongue, and did not reprove them for their sins, therefore they thought Him to be such a one as themselves, that He was a sinner as well as they. "Because sentence against an evil work is not speedily executed," therefore the hearts of the sons of men are set in them to do evil. The forbearance of God to wicked men makes them run on into practical atheism, whereas this is no ground at all to encourage them to run on in sin.

The forbearance of God's judgments was never intended by God to breed atheism in your heart, but to provoke you to repentance. As the apostle said, the bountifulness and long-suffering of God should lead us to repentance.

It will aggravate your condemnation to make the forbearance of God a provocation to you to go on in sin.

And know this: though God forbears awhile from punishing you for your sins, yet He neither forgives you nor forgets you. Nahum 1:3: "The Lord is slow to anger and great in power, and will not at all acquit the wicked." Though God forbears you, yet He will not forget you. So in Ecclesiastes 8:12: "Though a sinner do evil an hundred times, and his days be prolonged, yet surely I know that it shall be well with them that fear God."

2. Another ground whereby wicked men plunge themselves into atheism is because they see other men, who are knowing men, and professors of religion, men who pretend to know, love, and worship God, when wicked men see such men as these fall into great and gross sins, and

live so unanswerably to their profession, this makes them conclude that there is no God in the world. In Romans 2:24 the apostle says, "The name of God is blasphemed among the Gentiles through you." I have read a strange story of a woman here in England who called into question the Deity, whether there was a God or not. A minister came to convince her, and satisfy her conscience, and persuade her into a belief that there was a God. He asked her this question: How did you come to be an atheist?" She answered that very first thing that caused her to entertain thoughts of atheism, to believe there was no God, was seeing him, the minister, live so wickedly and profanely. Said she, "I know you to be a learned and knowing man, and you preach good sermons and exhort people well, and beholding you to live so wickedly, to be a swearer, a liar, a drunkard, and a Sabbath-breaker made me question whether there was a God in heaven or not, seeing that He let you run on still unpunished."

3. Another thing that makes men live as if there were no God in the world is the questioning of the authority of the Scriptures. I have read of one (a great scholar in this kingdom) that the means whereby he came to be an atheist was this: he first began to question whether the Bible was the Word of God or not because he did not know whether Moses, who penned the beginning of it, was a man of God or not. Then he questioned how Moses could write those things that were done before he was born, and then whether the papists might not alter it in the translating of it. There were many other questions he asked till, by degrees, he came to be an atheist, and to question whether there was a God or not.

And so there are some errors now in print that tend very much to atheism. There are some who affirm that the book or volume of books called the Bible is not the Word of God, and such an opinion as this greatly works upon men's hearts and persuades them that there is no God. In 2 Peter 3:3 the apostle says, "There shall come in the last days scoffers, walking after their own lusts." These are the atheists, but how came they to be so? Mark the next words:

"and saying, Where is the promise of His coming? For since the fathers fell asleep, all things continue as they were from the beginning." Say they, "We have heard that all men must be judged, that after death they must appear before the judgment-seat of God to give an account of all their actions." Now because they did not see these things accomplished already, they cried out, "Where is the promise of His coming?" They would not believe there was any such thing. The questioning of the truths of God was that which brought them to be very atheists.

4. Another ground from whence atheism flows is pride of heart. It is very well observed that most commonly atheists are of the greatest men. You shall seldom see a poor man an atheist, but rich men altogether. As Pharaoh said in Exodus 5:2: "Who is the Lord that I should obey His voice?" And so said Nebuchadnezzar in Daniel 3:15: "Who is that God that shall deliver you out of my hands?" Alexander said he himself was God. Atheists are ordinarily of the greatest, richest, and highest people.

OBJECTION. But here some may object and say, "What, do you tell us here in England that we are without God in the world? You may say so to pagans and heathens, but we hope you will not say so to us!"

ANSWER. For answer to this objection, I shall here show you thirteen marks of a practical atheist. I shall give you three of them out of Scripture, and ten more deduced from Scripture. In Psalm 14:1, where it is said, "The fool hath said in his heart there is no God," in that very psalm there are three discoveries of an atheist.

First, a man living all his days in a profane and disordered course of life towards God is an atheist. In the first verse of that same Psalm: "The fool hath said in his heart there is no God." What follows? "They are corrupt, they have done abominable works, there is none that doeth good." The man who all his lifetime lives in a disorderly course of life, and adds drunkenness to thirst, and commits one sin after another, that man is a practical atheist. He lives as if there were no God in the world.

Second, the man who wholly neglects the duty of

prayer is an atheist. Psalm 14:4: "They eat up my people as they eat bread, and call not upon the Lord." Such a man is a practical atheist.

Third, the man who hates and carries a grudge in his heart against those who fear the Lord is an atheist. Psalm 14:6: "Ye shamed the counsel of the poor, because the Lord is His refuge."

Now give me leave to press these three marks home upon your consciences. Are they atheists who live a disorderly life and walk in a course of wickedness all their days? Are such as these atheists? Oh, then, how many atheists are there now in the world who spend all their days in sin and vanity, and in a moment go down into the grave!

Are they atheists who neglect the duty of prayer? Oh, then, with grief of heart be it spoken, how many atheists are there in the world who wholly omit this duty, both in their families and in their closets? How many are there who can say they never go to God upon their knees in secret to beg for grace and mercy from God? And this neglect of secret duties is a palpable demonstration that you live as if there were no God in the world, and in so doing you are very atheists.

Is hatred and contempt of the people of God a badge of an atheist? Then likewise are there many atheists in the world. How many are there that can love a swearer, an adulterer, a profaner, yea, love a dog and yet hate a Christian? This proceeds from a root of atheism that is in their hearts.

16

Further Characteristics of an Atheist

"And without God in the world." Ephesians 2:12

I delivered to you in my last sermon three Scripture marks of an atheist. There are ten other characteristics left to be drawn from the Scriptures.

4. That man is an atheist who indulges and favors himself in the practice of secret sins. He who continually allows and favors himself in the practice of secret sins lives as if there were no God in the world. Reverend Mr. [William] Perkins gives us this badge of an atheist, that the very sin which he will not dare to commit in the presence of a child, that sin will he venture upon when no eye sees him. You who can venture upon a sin in hope of secrecy, thinking to hide it from the all-seeing eye of God, you are an atheist. You who dare do in the sight of God what you are afraid to do in the presence of a man, this proceeds merely from a root of atheism that is in the heart, as in Job 22:12–14. When a wicked man has done wickedly, he is ready to say, "How does God know? Can He judge through the thick clouds? Thick clouds are a covering to Him so that He does not see." These are the expressions of an atheistic heart. If an atheist can but keep himself from the censure and reproach of men, he is well enough. If men cannot say black to his eye, or there goes a drunkard, a swearer, an adulterer, or the like, he is never troubled for his sins. Oh, therefore, you who would be accounted chaste where you dwell, and yet keep your Delilah in your lap; and you debauched liver, who can quietly and securely walk on in ways of sin so that you can but keep them from the eyes of men, know this much: this proceeds from your atheistic heart. When the hope of se-

crecy emboldens any man to the practice of any sin, that man is a very atheist.

You who can fear the eye of a mortal man, and yet not be afraid of the all-seeing eye of an immortal God; you who were never troubled for your sins when nobody knew them but yourselves; now this is that which troubles you: your sins are known to others. If it is thus with you, you are a practical atheist. Those who are troubled not because God sees their sins, but because men see them, are very atheists, as in Job 24:13, 15, 17. These are they "that rebel against the light, they know not the ways thereof, nor abide in the path thereof. The eye also of the adulterer, waiteth for the twilight, saying, no eye shall see me, and disguiseth his face. For the morning is to them even as the shadow of death; if one knows them, they are in the terrors of the shadow of death." Such as these are very atheists; they were not troubled because God saw their sins, but because man saw their sins. This is as the terror of death to them. They would not have men see their sins, and yet they do not care what follies they are guilty of in the sight of God. So if man cannot say black to their eyes, they are well enough. Such men as indulge themselves in the practice of secret sins are practical atheists. A godly man will fear to commit a secret sin as well as a known gross and open sin. As Joseph said, "How shall I do this great wickedness and so sin against God?" If the apprehensions of God lie near your heart, you will have a care to avoid secret as well as open sins.

5. That man is a practical atheist who does not make conscience of the performance of secret duties. He who never prays in secret harbors the atheistic thought in him that God does not hear him. It is very observable of the Scribes and Pharisees in Scripture: you shall never read of a secret fast they kept, nor a private prayer they made, but they had a great many public fasts. They fasted twice a week, prayed in the corners of the streets, and gave alms, but you never read of any private and secret duties they performed, which proceeded merely from roots of atheism in their hearts. And so this is an evidence of the athe-

istic heart: if you never make conscience of going to God in secret and begging for grace and mercy from Him. He is an atheist who lives in the neglect of secret duties, for those men who retain in their hearts an apprehension of a Deity know there is no time so well spent, as that which is employed in secret prayer to God. Song of Solomon 2:14: "Oh, my dove (says Christ) that art in the clefts of the rock, in the secret places of the stairs: let me see thy countenance, let me hear thy voice, for sweet is thy voice, and thy countenance is comely." Oh, you poor soul (says Christ) who prays in secret, and weeps in secret corners, let Me see your face and hear your voice! A man who has the apprehensions of God before him knows that the Lord sees and takes notice of the breathings of his heart before Him in secret. And therefore, they are as much in the closet to pray in secret, and to pour out their souls before God in private, as they are in public.

It is very observable that there were very few actions of Christ that were recorded by all the four evangelists, and yet Christ's praying alone, when nobody was with Him, is recorded by them all; whereas other things, if they were recorded by one were left out by another. But this is spoken of by all of them. Now the reason of it is because Christ would be an example to us, to teach us to be frequent in the performance of this duty. And therefore it is a sign of an atheistic heart in anyone who does not make conscience of pouring out his heart in secret prayer to God.

6. The man who makes impunity to be a provocation to impiety is an atheist. My meaning is this: he who makes the patience and forbearance and long-suffering of God towards him to be a provocation to sin. Because God does not presently punish him for his sin, therefore he will go on in sin still. Such a man is an atheist. Psalm 50:21: "These things hast thou done (says God) and I kept silence; therefore thou thoughtest that I was altogether such an one as thyself." Beloved, if any of you harbor such thoughts as these in your hearts, that because God does not presently punish you for your sins, therefore you will

go on still in sin, let me tell you that this is the practice of a very atheist. Because the drunkard is not taken away by God while the wine is in his head; because the swearer is not destroyed by God while the oath is in his mouth; because the liar is not cut off by God while the lie is upon his tongue—therefore they will run on with greediness and willingness in the same sins. All this flows from the very root of atheism that is in your heart.

7. That man is an atheist who carries in his heart a forgetfulness and carelessness of the day of judgment. 2 Peter 3:3: "There shall come in the last days scoffers, walking after their own lusts, saying, Where is the promise of His coming?" You who do not harbor in your heart a mindfulness of the day of judgment are a very atheist, for you who do not believe God to be a judge do not believe Him to be a God. When Paul spoke to Felix of temperance, and of the judgment to come, his heart trembled at the hearing of it. Ecclesiastes 11:9: "Rejoice, O young man in thy youth, and let thy heart cheer thee in the days of thy youth, and walk in the ways of thine heart, and in the sight of thine eyes; but know thou that for all these things God will bring thee to judgment." You who live in the world, and never so much as think of a day of judgment, you are a very atheist. And oh, beloved, how many atheists are there now in the world in this regard, who put far from them the evil day!

8. That man is a very atheist who, in the time of trouble and distress, mistrusts the providence of God and runs to base means for help and remedy. Thus Saul discovered himself to be an atheist in 1 Samuel 28:7–8. When he was in distress, he went to the witch of Endor for help and succor. And what did God say of such as run to witches and wizards: "Is it not because there is not a God in Israel, that you run to other gods to inquire of them?" It is mere atheism for any to distrust God and run to others for help, or any other way to run into sinful courses in times of danger to find relief. You hereby declare that you think there is no God in the world.

9. That man is an atheist who places his affections

upon anything in the world other than upon God. Such a man lives without God in the world. A covetous man who places his love upon his money more than upon anything in the world makes gold his god; and therefore these two are joined together in Ephesians 5:5: "The covetous person, who is an idolater." He makes an idol of his money. This Job frees himself from in Job 31:24–28: "I have not made gold my hope, nor fine gold my confidence, for, if I had done so, then I had denied the God above." Beloved, there are many among us who love money better than their own souls, who will sell their souls to gain a little wealth. Many among us love money more than we love heaven itself. They do not care what sins they commit for it, and would rather part with their souls than their riches. And so when you set your love upon your belly, you make your belly your god; or if upon pleasures, then you make pleasures your god; and so with anything else. And therefore, beloved, I beseech you look to it and examine yourselves: is not God undervalued sometimes when your lusts are set on the throne? Is not God sometime very low in your estimation, and other things set above Him? If it is so, it is mere atheism in your hearts.

10. That man is an atheist who makes no conscience of keeping those vows and covenants he has made with God. The Scripture looks upon that man as an atheist who does not make conscience of performing those covenants that he has made with God. Joshua 24:25–27: "So Joshua made a covenant with the people that day, and set them a statue and an ordinance in Shechem. And Joshua wrote these words in the book of the law of God, and took a great stone, and set it up there under an oak that was by the sanctuary of the Lord. And Joshua said unto all the people, 'Behold this stone shall be a witness unto us, for it hath heard all the words of the Lord which He spake unto us; it shall be therefore a witness unto you, lest ye deny your God.' " And therefore those men who call the covenant that we have made (with hands lifted up to the high God) an old almanac, out of date, and scorn and despise the oath they have taken, and make no conscience of

keeping the vows and covenants they have made with God, the Scripture looks upon such men as very atheists. Beloved, in this regard, there are more atheists now in England than ever there were since the world stood. But the Lord will manifest Himself to be a just God, though wicked men despise His covenant and count it as an unholy thing.

11. That man is a very atheist whose conscience never troubles nor checks him for the commission of any sin. The man who can be drunk today, swear tomorrow, cheat the next day, and commit one sin after another, and yet his conscience never give him any control, that man is a very atheist. Those who can live in the world and commit gross sins every day, and their consciences never check them for their sins, it is a sad sign that such men are practical atheists. If you have the fear of God in you, and the thoughts of God on you, it will make you reflect upon sins past, and be grieved for sins and miscarriages of twenty years standing. Thus did Joseph's brethren call to mind their former sins in Genesis 42:21: "And they said one to another, We are verily guilty concerning our brother, in that we saw the anguish of his soul, when he besought us, and we would not hear; therefore is this distress come upon us." So did Job: "Thou writest bitter things against me, and makest me to possess the iniquities of my youth." So David prayed that God would not remember the sins of his youth. But you who can be drunk one day after another, and belch out one oath after another, and commit one sin after another, and your conscience never control you, the Lord be merciful to you, for you are plunged into a depth of atheism. One compared an atheist to a duck in a pond: if a man throws a stone into the water where she is, she will presently dive under, but let it thunder or lightning never so much in the heavens she takes no notice of it. So an atheist cannot endure that men should take notice of him, or discover his wickedness to reprove him or speak against him, but let God thunder upon him never so much, he will not be troubled at it. If you lived under the apprehensions of a Deity, it would be impossi-

ble that your conscience should be so long and so frequently out of its office.

12. Those men are very atheists who yield to a detestable indifference in matters of religion. The man who will sleep in a whole skin, and not dare to do any thing to the hazarding of his estate or person for the advancement of true religion, such a man is a very atheist. I will give you a strange place for this. In 1 Kings 18:21 Elijah the prophet says to the people: "How long halt ye between two opinions? If the Lord be God, follow Him; but if Baal, then follow him." And the text says, "The people held their peace, and answered him not a word." They neither said they would follow after God, nor did they say they would follow after Baal. If God was too strong for Baal, they would be for God; but if Baal prevailed, they would follow after him; which manifested their atheism, and that God was not their God. The man who takes God to be his God must follow Him through whatever troubles or afflictions he meets with in the world. Indifference in matters of religion argues men to be very atheists. And therefore all timeservers, who live according to the times, who are men of indifferent tempers, any religion rather will serve their turns, such men are practical atheists.

13. Men show themselves to be atheists when their practices palpably thwart and contradict their professions, when they are such as those spoken of in Titus 1:16, that in their words do profess to know Christ, but in their works they deny him." Those who profess themselves to be Christians and yet live like heathens; who profess themselves to have an inheritance with the saints in light and yet walk here as children of darkness, such men are very atheists.

And thus I have done with these ten discoveries of a practical atheist. I have given you thirteen in all—three of them out of the Scripture and ten more deduced from the Scripture.

Application

USE OF COUNSEL. If it is so that all unregenerate men are practical atheists, they live as if there were no God in the world, oh, then, that you would bewail this practical atheism that is among you. Do you favor yourself in the practice of secret sins? Do you make no conscience of the performance of secret duties? Do you make impunity to be a provocation to impiety? Do you carry in thy mind a forgetfulness of the day of judgment? Do you distrust the providence of God in times of trouble and distress? Do you place your affections upon anything in the world more than upon God? Do you make no conscience of performing the vows and covenants you have made with God? Does your conscience never trouble you after the commission of sins? Are you a lukewarm and indifferent man in matters of religion? Do you profess to know God, but in your works deny Him? Do you in any of these ways entertain and harbor thoughts of atheism in your heart? Why, so far as you have done so, labor to bemoan and bewail it, and be humbled for it, and so strive against and keep under this great sin of atheism in time to come.

USE OF CONSOLATION. This shall be to comfort and support your hearts. It may be there are some of you who hear me this day who are the precious servants of God, and yet in some kind or other have been tempted to this sin of atheism. Well, for your comfort consider these two things.

Are you tempted to atheism? Why, yet consider that so was Jesus Christ Himself. He was tempted to atheism and blasphemy when the devil tempted Him to fall down and worship him. So, though you have been tempted to atheism, and to forget God's all-seeing eye over you, yet this may be for your comfort: Christ Himself was tempted as well as you. The apostle says, in Hebrews 2:18: "In that He Himself hath suffered and, being tempted, He is able to succor those that are tempted." Christ was tempted to fall down and worship the very devil, but, though Christ was tempted, yet the devil could find no corrupt matter in Christ to work upon. When the devil shook Christ, he shook a pure crystal glass of clear water. His nature was like a crystal glass full of clean water without any muddiness or corruption at all; but if the devil should shake any of us, he would find abundance of dirty and muddy water in the bottom, and corrupt matter enough in our natures to work upon.

Consider that, though you are tempted by the devil to the sin of atheism, yet these temptations, if you do not approve of them nor yield to them, shall be charged upon the devil as his sins and not upon you.

And thus you see I have briefly dispatched this doctrine, that every man by nature is a practical atheist, living in the world as if there were no God.

17

Wicked Men Have No Interest in God

"And without God in the world." Ephesians 2:12

Wicked men are without God in the world, that is, they are without any special interest or propriety in God as their God. The words do not only imply that they live as if there were no God in the world, but they live without any right, interest, or propriety in God as their God. Though they are not without wisdom or wealth, or goods and estate, or honor and esteem in the world, yet they are without any real interest or propriety in God as their God. They are without God in the world, from whence I would note you this doctrine:

DOCTRINE. Every man by nature is without any real interest or propriety in God as his God.

Now beloved, before I come to handle the point, I shall only premise three conclusions by way of explanation, to elucidate the point and show you what I mean by this doctrine.

1. Take this conclusion: in some sense there is no creature in the world that is without God, though in other regards men may be truly said to be without God. In some sense there are none without God, that is, by way of creation and preservation; so the worst devil in hell may say that God is his God.

A wicked man may have God to be his God by way of profession. He may profess to know God, and profess that God is his God; but in another sense a wicked man cannot be said to have God for his God, that is, in a way of relation and reconciliation, for God to be a God in covenant with him through Jesus Christ.

2. Take this conclusion: though multitudes of people

156

may lay claim to God as their God, yet there are but a few men in the world who have God to be their God in a covenant way. In Zechariah 13:8–9, the Lord looks upon the Jewish church under a threefold consideration. "And it shall come to pass that in all the land, saith the Lord, two parts therein shall be cut off and die, but the third shall be left therein, and I will bring the third part through the fire, and will refine them as silver is refined, and will try them as gold is tried; they shall call on My name and I will hear them; I will say, it is My people, and they shall say the Lord is my God." Though you all lay claim to God, yet there may be but one in three who can truly say that God is their God, and is in covenant with them.

3. Take this conclusion: such is the deceitfulness and delusion of men's hearts naturally that the worst of men are ready to believe and think that God is their God when He is not. You may read Jeremiah 3:4–5. God says there: "They shall cry unto Me, my Father, Thou art the guide of my youth." And yet, says God: "thou hast done evil as much as thou couldst." Psalm 14:1: "The fool hath said in his heart there is no God, they are corrupt and have done abominable works, there is none that doeth good." Those who do not have God in their hearts, nor in all their ways, will yet lay claim to God as their God, though they have committed abominable works, and done as much evil as they could.

This much for the conclusion. I come now to handle a practical question that necessarily must be spoken to in the pursuance of this doctrine.

QUESTION. What are the characters of those men who are without any real interest and propriety in God as their God, in a way of covenant and relation?

ANSWER. This question I rather resolve upon the consideration of the great delusion and mistake that men's hearts are very apt to run into, to think that God is their God when He is not; and therefore I shall lay down to you seven distinguishing characters of such men, and, it may be, I may come near the bosoms of many of you, though the Lord knows I would not stagger the hope of the least of you who have a real and well-grounded interest in Jesus Christ.

Those men are without any real interest in God as their God:

1. Who are without any effectual knowledge of God as their God.

2. Who live without making the Word of God to be their rule.

3. Who live in the world without making the ways of God to be their pleasure.

4. Who live in the world without making the glory of God to be their aim.

5. Who live in the world without making the day of the Lord to be their delight.

6. Who live in the world without making the people of God to be the objects of their love.

7. Who live in the world without making sin to be the object of their hatred.

I will now examine each of these:

1. *Those men are without any real interest in God as their God who are without any real interest or propriety in God as their God, who live in the world without a saving and effectual knowledge of God.* In 2 Chronicles 15:3 it is said there that, for a long time, "Israel hath been without the true God, and without a teaching priest, and without the law." All that time (while they were without the law, and the priest to teach them) it is said they were without God. Those who live without a saving knowledge of God are looked upon by Scripture as having no real interest in God. John 8:54–55: "You say (says Christ) that He is your God, yet you have not known Him," intimating that God was not their God because they were utterly ignorant of Him.

Now, beloved, every knowledge of God does not demonstrate your interest in God, unless it is a practical knowledge of Him. In John 8:55 Christ says, "I am of God, I know Him, and keep His sayings," intimating that the man who lays claim to God as his God must know Him;

and this knowledge of Him will make him yield obedience to Him and keep his sayings.

It must be an experimental knowledge of God. David says in Psalm 51:6: "Behold, Thou desirest truth in the inward parts; and in the hidden part Thou shalt make me to know wisdom." If you were persons living without a practical and experimental knowledge of God, you are without any interest in him as your God.

OBJECTION. Before I can leave this particular, I must answer an objection. I think I hear a poor perplexed soul say, "If this is so, that only those who know God aright have an interest in Him, then the Lord be merciful unto me, for I am a poor ignorant sinful wretch who knows nothing of God at all as I ought to know him. And, therefore, surely I have no interest in God as my God."

ANSWER. Now to such as you are, by way of answer, I shall leave these words for your comfort.

Take this for an answer: in Scripture account, to complain of your ignorance is a good degree of knowledge. In Proverbs 30:2–3 you read of Agur, who was an excellent man in virtue and knowledge in the time of Solomon; and yet you shall not read of a man who more complained of his ignorance than this man: "Surely I am more brutish than any man, and have not the understanding of a man: I neither learned wisdom, nor have attained to the knowledge of the holy." Yet this man, who complained so much of his ignorance, demonstrated such fruits of grace and knowledge in his practice as ever man did.

Take this for an answer: in God's account he knows most that does most. He does not know most who has a great judgment to dive into and dispute about vain questions and niceties, but he is a knowing man in God's account who walks answerably to the small measure of knowledge he has. Psalm 111:10: "A good understanding have all they that do His commandments." God does not measure your knowledge by your questions and disputes, but by your practice. Jeremiah 22:16: "He judged the cause of the poor and needy; then it was well with him. Was not this to know Me? saith the Lord?"

Take this for an answer: it is not the wanting of some measures or degrees of knowledge, nor the having of much ignorance, that demonstrates your want of an interest in God, unless your ignorance has these three properties with it:

First, suppose you are ignorant of God, yet if you are not conceitedly ignorant, if you are not a self-conceited man who thinks he knows much when he knows little, you are well enough—if you are not like those in Hosea 8:2: "Israel shall cry unto Me, 'My God, we know Thee,'" and yet there is no fear, nor knowledge of God in the land."

Second, if you do not sit down contentedly in your ignorance, but labor and endeavor after more knowledge, then your condition is good enough. But if you say unto God, "Depart from me, for I desire not the knowledge of Thy ways," like those spoken of in Job, this is a sad sign that you have no interest in God at all.

Third, if you are not obstinately ignorant, like those spoken of in Psalm 82:5: "They know not, neither will they understand." When men are ignorant, and will be ignorant, this is an evidence that they have no interest in God. In 2 Peter 3:5 the apostle says, "For this they are willingly ignorant." Now if your ignorance is accompanied with these three circumstances, that you are conceitedly and contentedly and obstinately ignorant, if so, the Lord be merciful to you. For these are apparent demonstrations that you have yet no interest and propriety in God as your God. But though you have an abundance of ignorance in you, yet if you bewail your ignorance, and labor and desire after more knowledge, if you follow on to know the Lord, and are not obstinately ignorant, but would do more if, you knew more, if it is thus with you, your ignorance does not evidence that you have no interest in God.

2. *Another character of a man who is without an interest in God is this: he is one who lives in the world without making the Word of God to be his rule.* John 8:47: "He that is of God, heareth God's words; ye therefore hear them not, because ye are not of God." Those who will not make the Word of God to be their rule, and conform their practices in obe-

dience thereunto, Christ says the reason is because they
are not of God. And so in 1 John 4:6: "He that knoweth
God, heareth us; and he that is not of God, heareth not
us." And therefore, you who walk after the vain imaginations of your own hearts, who are swayed and ruled by
your lusts, and will not make God's Word a bridle to curb
and restrain your lusts and corruptions, but will do what
you will, let God command what He will—all these are
manifest arguments that you are not of God.

3. *That man is without an interest in God who lives in the
world without making the ways of God to be his pleasure.* 1 John
3:10: "In this the children of God are manifest and the
children of the devil: whosoever doeth not righteousness
is not of God." Righteousness is not to be taken here only
for justice or civil righteousness, but for the whole bulk of
godliness and the body of Christianity. "He that doeth not
righteousness is not of God." Not doing righteousness is
answerable to committing sin. 1 John 3:8: "He that committeth sin is of the devil." Now this is not to be taken
simply to mean that he who falls into sin is of the devil,
but he who commits sin (that is) with complacency and
delight, and without any compulsion, such a man is of the
devil. So likewise, he who does not do righteousness is not
of God, that is, he who does not act and do it with delight,
alacrity, and complacency; such a one is not of God. In 3
John 1:11 the apostle says, "Beloved, follow not that which
is evil, but that which is good: he that doeth good is of
God; but he that doeth evil, hath not seen God." That is,
he who does evil with delight and satisfaction, he who
does not take delight in the ways of God and perform holy
duties with cheerfulness and complacency, such a man is
not of God. Therefore, you who take more delight in the
committing of sin than you do in the performance of holy
duties are in a bad condition.

4. *Another character is this: that man is without God who
lives in the world without making the glory of God to be his aim.*
It is very observable that when the Jews accused Christ,
saying that He was a Samaritan and had a devil, and did
not come from God, He convinced them that this was a

slander cast upon Him, because He sought not His own
honor, but the glory of God. In John 8:49–50 Jesus answered: "I have not a devil, but I honor My Father, and ye
do dishonor Me; and I seek not Mine own glory, there is
one that seeketh and judgeth."

5. *That man is without an interest in God who lives in the
world without making the day of God his delight.* He who takes
no delight in sanctifying the Lord's Day, but rather takes
delight in profaning it, that man is without God in the
world. In John 9:16 it was the speech of the Pharisees to
Christ: "This man is not of God, because He keepeth not
the Sabbath day." This would have been a very good argument, had it been rightly applied. The argument would
have been very strong if the application had been good, if
Christ had not indeed kept the Sabbath, but they were
greatly mistaken, for Christ *did* keep the Sabbath. Why,
now beloved, these Pharisees, were they now alive, and
should see you Christians profaning the Sabbath day,
spending and trifling it away in sports and pleasures, in
swearing and drunkenness, and dishonoring the name of
God; never employing one hour of it in prayer, reading,
or hearing, or any holy and religious exercise, they would
presently conclude that you are not of God, because you
do not keep the Sabbath.

6. *That man is without God who lives without making the
people of God to be the object of his love.* You may see this in 1
John 3:10: "Whosoever doeth not righteousness is not of
God, neither he that loveth not his brother." And so in 1
John 4:20: "If any man say, I love God, and hateth his
brother, he is a liar, for he that loveth not his brother
whom he hath seen, how can he love God whom he hath
not seen?" He who does not love his brother, the children
and people of God, cannot love God. You who carry in
your hearts a secret malice and spleen against those who
are godly, and more holy and religious than yourselves:
you who, tiger-like, hate the very pictures of godly men,
you who hate the people and the ministers of the gospel
because they are so, who hate godliness as godliness, these
are evident arguments that the love of God is not in you.

7. *That man is without God who lives in the world without making sin to be the object of his hatred.* That man has not God who hates not sin. Though that man may have God who has sin, yet that man cannot have an interest in God who does not hate sin.

And thus I have run over briefly these seven headings whereby you may know whether you are the men who can lay a true claim to God as your God or not. If you are men who have a true knowledge of God, and make His Word your rule and His way your pleasure, and His day your delight, and His glory your aim, and good men the object of your love, and sin the object of your hatred—if these things are in you, you may know undoubtedly that you have an interest in God.

Application

We come now to the application, which may serve for unspeakable comfort to all you who are the people of God, who can lay a well-grounded and Scripture claim to God as your God.

1. If you have God, you have all things. And let me tell you, you who have God for your God, you may outvie all the kings, princes, and potentates in the world. Other men may say they have wealth, and you have none; they have riches, honors, and pleasures, and you have none; but you may go further and outvie them all, for you can say that you have an interest in God and they have none. Wicked men cannot lay claim to God as theirs; and therefore when they speak of God, they speak of Him as a God to others and not to them. In Genesis 31:29, Laban spake to Jacob: "The God of your fathers." And so Pharaoh says in Exodus 8:25, 28: "Go ye, sacrifice to your God in the land." And from hence divines observe that the Scriptures do not allow wicked men to name God, in a way of propriety to them, as their God. But those who are righteous and holy, who indeed have an interest in God, God is not ashamed to be called their God. You who have an interest

in God, though you are a poor, despicable people, yet do not be afraid to own God as your God, for the Lord is not ashamed that you should call Him your God. God is not ashamed of us whose dwellings are in the dust. He will own us, and therefore let this encourage you to go to God as your God, and apply to Him as your God, and trust in Him as your God, and pray to Him and call upon Him as your God, for He is not ashamed of you.

And here, that I may speak a little further to this particular, I would exhort you to two things: first, to prove your interest in God; second, to improve it.

First, labor to prove your interest in God. Examine and try whether or not, upon conscientious grounds and Scripture evidences, your hearts can be satisfied that you are a people in covenant with God. Rest not, and trust not upon maybe's, but labor to prove to your own souls that God is your God. And that I may help and further you in this examination, I shall here lay down three discoveries whereby you may know and prove unquestionably that God is your God.

• If you are one who labors to keep your inward man from secret defilement by sin as well as your outward man, from grosser and greater enormities, as in 2 Corinthians 6:18, and in verse 1 of the next chapter: "I will be a Father unto you, and ye shall be My sons and daughters, saith the Lord God Almighty. Having therefore these promises, dearly beloved, let us cleanse ourselves from all filthiness, of the flesh and spirit"; and therefore, if you have a care to abstain from all secret sins whereby the inward man is defiled, it is a sign that you have a real interest in God, because God will be our God, and will own and accept us as His people. We must not only wash our legs and our outward man, but our inward parts too; and if we do this we may be confidently assured that we are a sacrifice well-pleasing and acceptable unto God through Jesus Christ. But you who make conscience of your ways so far only that men may not say black to your eye, if you do not labor to keep your inward man from defilements as well as your outward man, you have no interest in God at all.

• Another evidence of your interest in God is this: if you have an earnest and unwearied labor and endeavor in your spirits to come to the nearest resemblance and conformity to Jesus Christ as possibly as you can. Do you labor to be holy as He was holy? Do you labor to be humble, meek, and lowly as He was? In 2 Corinthians 7:1 the apostle says, "Dearly beloved, let us cleanse ourselves from all filthiness of flesh and spirit, perfecting holiness in the fear of God." Do you labor still to resemble God in holiness? Your relation and interest in God will make you labor to be like God, and to be still perfecting holiness, though you cannot be perfect in holiness. If you have an interest in God, you will labor more and more to be holy as He is holy, and to come to the nearest resemblance to Him that may be.

• Another discovery of your interest in God is this: if God has engraven upon your soul those saving effects and blessings which He bestows upon all those who have an interest in Him. God has promised that He will be their God, and they shall be His people; that He will give them a new heart; taking away the heart of stone and giving them a heart of flesh; that He will sanctify and renew their natures, and write His law in their inward parts; that He will work in their hearts a suitable disposition to His law, and put His fear into their hearts so that they shall never depart from Him. These are the blessings of the covenant of grace. Now you who can give abundant and evident testimonies in your own souls that you have found God cleansing and purifying your hearts, sanctifying and renewing your natures, writing His law in your inward parts, and putting His fear into your hearts so that you never depart from Him; if you find these things in you, they are undoubted evidences that you have an interest in God.

Second, as I would have you prove your interest in God, so I would exhort you to *im*prove your interest in God too. Many of you let God lie by you (as I may so say), and never make use of Him for your spiritual comfort and support, and never go to Him for help and succor and relief in times of danger. You do not improve your interest in God.

But here, it may be, you would ask me how you should improve your interest in God?

I answer, first, improve it by making your interest in God a great incitement and provocation to you to obey God. Thus David did in Psalm 143:10: "Teach me to do Thy will, for Thou art my God." Here David well improved his interest in God. So in Psalm 119:115: "Depart from me, ye evildoers, for I will keep the commandments of my God." We should make our interest in God an engagement upon our souls to keep the commands of God.

Second, you rightly improve your interest in God when this stirs you up to aggravate all the sins you have committed against God, when your interest in God makes you see how exceedingly sinful sin is, and how greatly you have provoked the Lord your God by your sins. Jeremiah 3:25: "We have sinned against the Lord our God, we and our fathers from our youth even to this day, and have not obeyed the voice of the Lord our God." Here the children of Israel aggravated their sins against God as their God. And so Daniel made his interest in God a motive to stir him up to aggravate sin against God. In Daniel 9:5 he says, "We have sinned, and have committed iniquity, and have done wickedly, and have rebelled, even by departing from Thy precepts, and from Thy judgments." And then in verse 7: "O Lord, righteousness belongeth unto Thee, but unto us confusion of faces, as at this day." So again in verses 8–9: "O Lord, to us belongeth confusion of face, to our kings, and to our princes, and to our fathers, because we have sinned against Thee. To the Lord our God belongth mercy and forgiveness, though we have rebelled against Him." And so he goes on all along, aggravating their sins against God. No less than ten times he mentions their interest in God, and ten times he aggravates their sins against God. It is the consideration of our interest in God that stirs us up to aggravate our sins against God, when we consider that we have sinned against our God, against our gracious and merciful Father who has loved us and given us everlasting consolation and good hope through grace, who is infinite in goodness and abundant in mercy and truth. Such considerations as these will exceedingly provoke us to aggravate our sins against Him.

Third, improve your interest in God by making it a prop and pillar of marble to bear up and support your hearts under all the miseries, afflictions, and troubles you meet with here in the world. Thus David encouraged himself in the Lord his God in Psalm 3:7: "Arise, O Lord; save me, O my God." You make a right improvement of your interest in God when you go to Him, and trust and rely and depend upon Him in all times of danger and distress; for you have an interest in that God who is both able and willing to relieve and succor you, a God who has helped you, and does help you, and will never leave you nor forsake you. Therefore be encouraged to cast your care upon Him.

Finis